18
26

99 Ablex

Library Performance, Accountability, and Responsiveness

Essays in Honor of Ernest R. DeProspo

INFORMATION MANAGEMENT, POLICY, AND SERVICES

Charles R. McClure and Peter Hernon, Editors

Library Performance Accountability and Responsiveness: Essays in Honor of Ernest R. DeProspo
> *Charles C. Curran and F. William Summers*

Curriculum Initiative: An Agenda and Strategy for Library Media Programs
> *Michael B. Eisenberg and Robert E. Berkowitz*

Resource Companion to Curriculum Initiative: An Agenda and Strategy for Library Media Programs
> *Michael B. Eisenberg and Robert E. Berkowitz*

The Role and Importance of Managing Information for Competitive Positioning in Economic Development
> *Keith Harman*

A Practical Guide to Managing Information for Competitive Positioning in Economic Development
> *Keith Harman*

Microcomputer Software for Performing Statistical Analysis: A Handbook for Supporting Library Decision Making
> *Peter Hernon and John V. Richardson (Editors)*

Public Access to Government Information, Second Edition
> *Peter Hernon and Charles R. McClure*

Statistics for Library Decision Making: A Handbook
> *Peter Hernon et al.*

U.S. Government Information Policies: Views and Perspectives
> *Charles R. McClure, Peter Hernon and Harold C. Relyea*

U.S. Scientific and Technical Information Policies: Views and Perspectives
> *Charles R. McClure and Peter Hernon*

In preparation

Power, Politics, and Personality: The State Library Agency as a Policy Actor
> *June Engle*

Microcomputer Graphics as a Library Resource
> *Bradford S. Miller*

Investigations of Human Responses to Knowledge Representations
> *Mark E. Rorvig*

Technology and Library Information Services
> *Carol Anderson and Robert Hauptman*

Library and Information Skills Instruction in Elementary Schools
> *Michael B. Eisenberg and Robert E. Berkowitz*

Library and Information Skills Instruction in Secondary Schools
> *Michael B. Eisenberg and Robert E. Berkowitz*

Microcomputer Local Area Networks and Communications
> *Thomas R. Kochtanek and Frederick J. Raithel*

LIBRARY PERFORMANCE, ACCOUNTABILITY, AND RESPONSIVENESS

ESSAYS IN HONOR OF ERNEST R. DEPROSPO

Edited by

Charles C. Curran

and

F. William Summers

ABLEX PUBLISHING CORPORATION
NORWOOD, NEW JERSEY

Library of Congress Cataloging-in-Publication Data

Library performance, accountability, and responsiveness : essays in
    honor of Ernest R. DeProspo / edited by Charles C. Curran with the
    assistance of F. William Summers.
          p.   cm.—(Information management, policies, and services)
    Includes bibliographical references.
    ISBN 0–89391–597–1
    1. Libraries—Evaluation.   2. Library administration.
    3. Deprospo, Ernest R., 1937–   . I. Deprospo, Ernest R., 1937– 1983
    II. Curran, Charles C., 1934–   . III. Summers, F. William
    (Frank William), 1933–   . IV. Series.
Z678.85.L54   1990
025.1–dc20   89–78242
                                                                  CIP

Ablex Publishing Corporation
355 Chestnut St.
Norwood, NJ 07648

This collection of essays is dedicated to the memory of our friend and mentor Ernest R. DeProspo, Jr.
Also, with love to Joyce, Scott, and Diana DeProspo.
And to Carlisa.

Table of Contents

Preface

In 1984, Bill Summers and I had the idea to ask a number of the late Ernest DeProspo's friends to help put together a collection of essays that would pay tribute to him and help establish at Rutgers a fund to be used to honor his memory and to further the kinds of causes he championed.

This volume represents the culmination of the effort to assemble essays which, while paying tribute to DeProspo, stand on their own merits as statements about libraries and research, and about performance and accountability, two of his passions.

In addition to the important ideas presented by the authors of these papers, two messages leap from these pages. One is the profound influence of DeProspo upon the thinking of the persons with whom he associated. The other is esteem and affection for the man and his ideas.

The contributions to this project reveal not only the impact of DeProspo's influence upon his students and friends but also the significant way in which his thought has impacted the information professions at large.

Charles Curran
January 1989

Acknowledgments

First, to the contributing authors: Thank you for your interest in this project. You have been willing, patient, and supportive. Charles R. McClure, thank you for your marketing advice. Ablex, thank you for believing in this project. Gayle Sykes, you are a heaven-sent editorial assistant: Special thanks to you. Catherine Mikan, thank you for your proofreading. Mimi Curlee, thank you for your indexing help.

Introduction

From her vantage point as Director of the American Library Association Office for Research, Mary Jo Lynch has a good view of research and research activity. Her chapter "The Measurement of Library Output" is a nicely stated encapsulation of the last 18 years' worth of research on measurement and planning of library services. Her account of current controversy does justice to those arguments and helps make her contribution an ideal leadoff essay.

Who better to report and reflect upon the impact of performance measurement than one who was part of the movement? In Chapter 2, "Reflections on Performance Measures Fifteen Years Later," Ellen Altman, partner with DeProspo in the Performance Measures project, does just what the title says: She reflects. What an interesting perspective she shares. She pulls no punches when she suggests some of the project's shortcomings, nor does she shy away from asserting its continuing positive impact on current efforts to plan and measure library performance.

One of the leaders of those current efforts is Charles R. McClure, author of Chapter 3—"Integrating Performance Measures into the Planning Process." He acknowledges the influence and contributions of DeProspo while asserting that Decision Support Systems are needed to help managers make fuller use of the tools at their disposal. He supplies a conceptual framework for doing so.

Chapter 4, "Aspects of Validity in Unobtrusive Studies," is contributed by Terence Crowley, one of the pioneers, along with Thomas Childers, in the study of reference service. It is fitting that his question: "Are we studying what we say we are?" should be considered early in this volume. Crowley not only thinks we are, but asserts that we must continue to do so as long as we hold that library service is important to all.

Thomas Childers asks another question in Chapter 5: "Do Library Systems Make a Difference?" *Yes,* he claims, citing the results of a recently conducted study in Pennsylvania. But he adds that it is imperative that we go in search of relationships between outcomes and systems participation, for true measures of accountability depend upon discovering those relationships.

In Chapter 6, "Public Libraries: Flexibility and Political Action," veteran public library director and library consultant Edwin Beckerman provides the perspective of the practitioner who has managed to find a solid balance between theory and practice. His message concerning community character, service goals, and political action is a sage one, and his claim is that in the tools provided by DeProspo and The Public Library Association we have assistance in the search for custom-tailored service and the methods for reporting our achievements.

Shirley Fitzgibbons narrows the focus in Chapter 7, subtitled "Providing Library Services for Children and Young Adults." Her essay chronicles the recent history of performance and planning activities, documents the absence of the measurement of library services to youth, and speaks encouragingly about the work of advocates such as Mary K. Chelton, and also about current efforts to address the problem of measuring youth services.

Thomas C. Phelps examines accountability from his perspective as Program Officer for the National Endowment for the Humanities. His Chapter 8, "The Accountability of Public Organizations for Projects Supported by Grant-Making Agencies," is a call for seekers of funds to include in their proposals the kinds of objectives which describe measurable outcomes and from which some good or benefit can be reasonably inferred. While hardly a primer on grantsmanship, the essay is valuable reading for proposal writers, especially any who are considering contact with The National Endowment for the Humanities, and it clearly reflects the influence of DeProspo, with whom Phelps worked when the performance measurement instruments were being tested.

"Accountability in the Classroom" is addressed by Charles Curran in Chapter 9. Lest the reader think DeProspo, an accomplished teacher as well as an expert researcher, viewed the role of educator as that of a middleman, Curran disposes of that interpretation and sketches a model, or more accurately, lists some ingredients which ought to become part of a mode for measuring the accountability of library educators. He also reports that DeProspo questioned the parentage of anyone insensitive enough to attempt to "measure springtime."

Barbara Williams Jenkins, an academic library director, addresses the issue of staff development in Chapter 10. She details the influence of the new technology on libraries, especially as it creates a need for updating skills and acquiring new ones. She sees a solution to the problem of providing such opportunities in a coalition of interested parties: educational agencies and associations.

Alan Samuels will bring readers into DeProspo's office for a discussion. Chapter 11, "Nontraditional Perspectives to Traditional Library Research," is a thought piece, rich in ideas and laced with the kinds of speculation that would have intrigued the Professor. Critical theory is the centerpiece of the Samuels essay. DeProspo would have poked at it and challenged its usefulness in measurement. So will readers of Chapter 11.

"Roads Not Taken: Some Thoughts about Librarianship" is the title of Chapter 12, contributed by F. William Summers, who went on from Rutgers to become dean at two library schools, the president of both The Association for Library and Information Science Education and The American Library Association. His observations are bound to stir debate, especially about librarianship's apparent decision to emphasize inventory control at the expense of information transfer. His chapter offers a generous portion of insightful comments and probing questions.

Chapter 13 is a special chapter. The task of sharing his personal experiences with Ernest DeProspo was assigned to Phil Clark who worked with him at Penn State and Rutgers and who was his close friend. "Biographical Sketch" is more than just a personal reminiscence, however. It reveals so much about Ernie the man. It is a disclosure about ideals and idealism. It shows the human side of Ernie, hints at what made him angry, and displays what drove him. Clark can be excused if he sides with his mentor on the performance measurement controversy and when he suggests that current planning processes have yet to achieve the handle on outcomes that performance measures showed so much promise for accomplishing. If Samuels drew us into Ernie's office for a discussion, Clark lays down some of the parameters for that discussion, which, if Ernie had anything to do with it, would include McClure and Altman, would evolve into a heated but friendly confrontation, and would last into the wee hours of the morning.

Curran offers in Chapter 14 a look at "A Future for Performance, Accountability, and Responsiveness." He would have eavesdropped on that discussion/confrontation mentioned above, thought about it for 17 years, and written the chapter. He sides with the planners and with planning processes, seeing them as logical extensions of what DeProspo fought for, and likely methods, if more fully developed, for achieving and demonstrating accountability.

Epilogue is a speech delivered by an actor at play's end. Usually that's what it is. Not here. Here it is a concluding piece on our mentor and friend. Clark called him a "sly jester." Was he ever!

Charles Curran
January 1989

1

Measurement of Library Output: How Is It Related to Research?

Mary Jo Lynch

Office for Research
   American Library Association
   Chicago, IL

SOME KEY MONOGRAPHS

Two books come to mind when I think about Ernest R. DeProspo. One is a book he used in the Rutgers doctoral seminar on research—Abraham Kaplan's (1964) *The Conduct of Inquiry*. In the doctoral seminar we read Kaplan closely, discussed it, wrote papers about key ideas, and used those ideas to draft our first research proposal. The second book I associate with Dr. DeProspo is *Performance Measures for Public Libraries* (DeProspo, Altman, & Beasley, 1973), the book which reported on a Public Library Association (PLA)-sponsored, Office of Education-funded project he directed that investigated new ways of measuring the effectiveness of public libraries. This chapter will comment on the connection between those two books and will also explore the relationship between scientific research and the development of tools for improving the management of public libraries.

Research is a word with many different meanings in the world at large and in the world of librarianship. In another paper (Lynch, 1984) I have suggested that at least four different activities called research are important to librarianship—practical research, bibliographical research, scholarly research, and scientific research. Kaplan was concerned primarily with only one of them, scientific research, as his subtitle indicated: *The Conduct of Inquiry* was about *Methodology for Behavioral Science*.

Until reading Kaplan, I had never thought much about scientific research. Like many librarians I had majored in English and equated research with going to the library to identify published material on a topic in order to write a term paper. Studying Kaplan opened a new world to me; I learned that scientific research involved disciplined gathering of facts in order to answer questions, thereby adding to the

1

sum total of human knowledge. Kaplan was anything but rigid about what was legitimate in scientific inquiry, but he did insist that new knowledge about reality is its goal and that logic and discipline are essential to the process.

The Conduct of Inquiry included a whole chapter on measurement. Kaplan believed it was important to recognize both what can be measured and what cannot be measured, to avoid both the "mystique of quality" (nothing worth talking about can be measured at all) and the "mystique of quantity" (everything worth talking about can be measured exactly). Kaplan also believed it was possible to measure almost anything as long as one was imaginative enough to think of ways to capture something meaningful about the phenomena in question and realistic enough to recognize that something is not everything. As Kaplan (1964) put it "whether we can measure something depends, not on that thing, but on how we have conceptualized it, on our knowledge of it, above all on the skill and ingenuity which we can bring to bear on the process of measurement . . . "(p. 127). It was this mindset which DeProspo brought to the work which resulted in *Performance Measures for Public Libraries*.

Traditionally, public libraries have been described and compared in terms of population served or budget size or items circulated. In the 1960s and 1970s, however, many people began to believe that such statistics were inadequate at a time when public libraries, like other public service institutions, were being held accountable not just for using funds honestly, but also for the efficient and effective delivery of services which were wanted and needed by the community. Accountability is difficult in the public sector because there are no obvious measures of effectiveness similar to private sector concepts like profit and return on investment. Although many librarians argued that it was impossible to measure what libraries provide, DeProspo believed it could be done.

THE DePROSPO INFLUENCE

What DeProspo and his colleagues did in the "Measurement of Effectiveness of Public Library Service Study" was to explore ways to measure something that had not been measured before—what a public library delivers to the community it serves—so that public library managers would have new tools to use in planning and evaluating their services. *Performance Measures for Public Libraries* was a report on the first two phases of the study, which was never completed. The report included a review of previous attempts to quantify library performance, an extended analysis of the problem, and a presentation of preliminary results. How does work on such a practical matter as measures for library managers relate to *The Conduct of Inquiry*? In what ways is it an appropriate activity for a team of people who believed in scientific methodology and were attached to a Bureau of Library and Information Science Research?

Kaplan believed that almost anything could be measured. He also accepted the legitimacy of research related to practical matters, which inevitably involve the behavior of people and the institutions people have created. In *The Conduct of Inquiry* Kaplan conveyed a belief that although the behavioral sciences were quite different from the physical and biological sciences in their ability to gain "hard" knowledge about reality, disciplined inquiry was definitely possible in behavioral matters. He explained how concepts underlying the more rigorous and well-established sciences could be incorporated into behavioral studies. Kaplan also believed that it was a legitimate use of a researcher's time to apply those concepts to solving practical problems. As he (Kaplan, 1964) phrased it "the fact is that the distinction between 'pure' and 'applied' science, whatever its logical ground, is not of much help in understanding the growth of knowledge" (p. 398).

As a student of Kaplan, DeProspo certainly understood the difference between a development project, which he was directing in the "Measurement of Public Library Effectiveness Study," and the research methodology he was teaching in his doctoral seminar. But he also recognized that both library managers and library researchers require effective tools for measuring what happens in libraries. Developing tools which are valid and reliable is a task to which scientific researchers bring several useful characteristics:

1. An ability to comprehend and criticize previous analytical work (e.g., Chapter 2 in reviews previous studies of library phenomena, primarily theoretical and mathematical, by systems analysts and operations researchers).
2. knowledge of analytical techniques used elsewhere in scientific work (e.g., the critique of U. S. Office of Education statistics in Chapter 3 of *Performance Measures* used multiple regression and significance testing, and the suggested approach to performance measurement relies on sampling, simulation, and calculation of probabilities).
3. The skills of disciplined observation and logical analyses.

Researchers are uniquely qualified to develop valid and reliable measurement tools and, once developed, these tools could be used not

only for management but also for scientific research into the phenomena of library use. Such tools have not yet been perfected, but
DeProspo started asking the questions which may make that possible
in the future.

Although there was much interest in the public library community
generally after *Performance Measures* was published, few researchers
seemed interested in examining the measures seriously. There *were*
two studies (Lynch, 1983) by research bureaus connected with
schools of library and information science which employed the measures statewide and recommended changes in procedure—one in New
Jersey and one in Illinois. These statewide studies focused on procedures for collecting data, however, and did not seriously test the
validity or reliability of the measures.

The measures recommended by DeProspo were never really tested
and were not widely adopted, but the idea of measuring libraries in
this way did not die. Almost 10 years later the public library community tried again to develop practical tools for measuring public library
output. Again PLA asked researchers to direct the work (Douglas
Zweizig and Eleanor Jo Rodger of King Research, Inc.), but the process of developing the measures and the resulting publication were
quite different. Instead of being conceptualized and operationalized
by researchers and tested in libraries in a federally-funded project,
the new measures were conceptualized by practitioners on a PLA
committee and operationalized and tested by researchers in a project
funded and directed by practitioners. Instead of a report on an un-
finished project, the second attempt produced a practical manual of
procedures (Zweizig & Rodger, 1982).

Because of DeProspo's work, the authors of *Output Measures for
Public Libraries* (OMPL) could start at a different place. They did not
have to study previous work or analyze existing statistics or explain
the theoretical base for what they were doing. Instead they described
a data collection methodology in clear and simple terms. This time
the methodology was used in many places (Owen, 1985) and, what is
more important, researchers started asking serious questions about
the validity and reliability of the measures (D'Elia, 1983; Van House,
1983).

After several years of experience with OMPL, PLA responded to the
criticisms of practitioners and researchers by commissioning a revi-
sion of the manual. The work was done by a team of researchers as
part of the Public Library Development Program which also produced
Planning and Role Setting in Public Libraries and the design for a
Public Library Data Service (Balcolm, 1986). The second edition of
Output Measures for Public Libraries (OMPL2) presents the same

twelve measures as the first, but gives more detailed instructions for collecting data and interpreting results (Van House, Lynch, McClure, & Zweizig, 1987).

The appearance of OMPL2 has not stopped debate among researchers but has intensified and expanded it, as can be seen in the Spring 1988 issue of *Public Libraries* which published articles by George D'Elia and Nancy Van House under the collective heading "The Usefulness of Fill Rates: Research and Debate." These two researchers continued the debate begun in earlier articles and added new insights to their respective positions. At issue are the three materials availability measures—author and title fill rate, subject fill rate, and browsers fill rate—which OMPL and OMPL2 recommend for measuring the extent to which a public library can meet the demands placed on it (Usefulness, 1988).

D'Elia is first with an eloquent presentation of his sophisticated analysis of data collected from material availability surveys in three systems—Saint Paul Public Library (Minnesota), Fairfax County Public Library (Virginia), and Baltimore County Public Library (Maryland). D'Elia concludes that whether one considers differences in the fill rates among branches in each of the three systems or among the three systems as collective entities, the differences are statistically significant (using Chi square), but trivial (using Cramer's V). The observed variations, therefore, are not due to any "diagnostically meaningful differences" among the libraries, but to unexplained variation in patron behavior. In addition, the fill rates are not related to other measures such as amount of resources available within the libraries or amount of use. D'Elia concludes that managers should be very careful in using fill rates to analyze the performance of a given library or to compare branches within systems or systems of libraries.

Van House responds by accepting D'Elia's point that the fill rates measure patron behavior as well as library performance and by noting that this is an important concept to bear in mind when using fill rates. She also agrees with him that managers should use the data with caution. But she argues strongly that he is premature in rejecting the fill rates completely when data from only three systems are available. Van House argues that these measures do have value and that the only way to improve the measures is to use and test them.

In the two final pieces in this cluster, D'Elia answers Van House and Van House answers D'Elia. D'Elia grants Van House's point that continued research is necessary, but he warns that "managers must recognize the apparent unreliability of fill rate data as we now understand it" (Usefulness, 1988, p. 29). Van House concludes by reassuring the nonresearcher that this kind of debate is common in research circles, though it usually takes place outside of publications for the practitioner. She advises the library manager to use fill rates, but only in connection with everything else that manager knows about the library and its uses and she cautions against using fill rates to make major financial decisions.

This kind of debate would have pleased DeProspo very much. He would have observed that his idea of studying the availablilty of items within a library as a measure of library performance has now been operationalized and used to the extent that data are available for study by researchers. He would have further observed that researchers are using systematic and objective inquiry, including statistical analysis, to evaluate the usefulness of a tool proposed for managers. It would not bother DeProspo that the matter is still unsettled. Like Kaplan (1964), he knew that "the scientist is in no hurry for closure" (p. 71).Tolerance of ambiguity is as important for creativity in science as it is anywhere else.

Another researcher (Rubin, 1986) has studied a different output measure in-depth—in-house use of materials. The Coalition for Public Library Research funded a study of this measure by the Library Research Center of the Graduate School of Library and Information Science Research at the University of Illinois. From the fall of 1984 to the fall of 1985, Richard Rubin and others collected data from nine library agencies on in-library use of materials by adults and children on a sample basis; studied alternative methods for measuring in-library use; and correlated in-house use with more easily measured variables.

The final report concluded that the methodology recommended in OMPL underrepresents the amount of in-house use of materials and recommends instead that patron questionnaires be used. In addition to yielding a higher figure for in-house use, the questionnaires also gather descriptive information about users. No matter what method is used, however, it is not possible to predict in-house use from more easily measured variables (e.g., visitor count, external circulation). Therefore, in-house use should be measured directly. The Rubin study was completed while OMPL2 was being produced and the study team working on it considered the recommendation that patron interviews be submitted for table counts. They decided, however, to stick with the table counts in the belief that the patron questionnaire method does not necessarily yield more valid or reliable data and may have the additional drawbacks of requiring more staff time and of annoying users.

The debate goes on and seems likely to continue. At this point it seems clear that effective measures of output for use in library management have not yet been achieved. It seems likely, however, that this will happen at some future date because the problem has engaged the attention of persons and groups who combine skill in research with an understanding of practice. This is happening not only in the public library community but also among academic librarians. Several years ago the Association of Research Libraries published *Objective Performance Measures for Academic and Research Libraries* in which Paul Kantor (1984) uses his earlier theoretical work in operations research to design methods whereby academic librarians can measure the library's performance. Kantor frequently quotes his own and others' research in explaining the recommended methodologies which incorporate sampling, simulation, and other techniques used in scientific data analysis. More recently, the Association of College and Research Libraries has contracted with Nancy Van House for a manual of procedures to be used by academic librarians to measure library output. Her previous work on public library output measures will probably influence the academic manual. Use of that manual, in turn, could lead to new insights into the problems of library measurement and accountability.

In the spirit of Abraham Kaplan, Ernest R. DeProspo used his understanding of scientific research principles to design a methodology for solving a practical problem. DeProspo was not entirely successful, nor have others solved the problem completely. Because of this work, however, the disciplined and objective methods of scientific research have been applied in a realistic way to the practical problem of measuring library output. Eventually library managers will have valid and reliable tools which can help them make decisions and demonstrate accountability. Those tools may also be used by researchers in the future to discover new knowledge about how libraries and other information services interact with their communities.

REFERENCES

Balcolm, Kathleen Mehaffy. (1986). The promise of the public library development project 'To concentrate and strengthen.' *Library Journal, 111*, 36–40.

D'Elia, George. (1983). Materials availability fill rates—Useful measures of library performance? *Public Libraries, 24*, 106–110.

DeProspo, Ernest, Altman, Ellen, & Beasley, Kenneth. (1973). *Performance measures for public libraries.* Chicago: American Library Association.

Kantor, Paul. (1984). *Objective performance measures for academic and research libraries.* Washington, DC: Association of Research Libraries.

Kaplan, Abraham. (1964). *The conduct of inquiry: Methodology for behavioral science*. New York: Harper & Row.

Lynch, Mary Jo. (1983). Measurement of public library activity: The search for practical methods. *Wilson Library Bulletin, 57*, 390.

Lynch, Mary Jo. (1984). Research and librarianship: An uneasy connection. *Library Trends, 32*, 367–371.

Owen, Amy. (1985). Output measures and state library development: A national survey. *Public Libraries, 24*, 98–101.

Rubin, Richard. (1986). *In-house use of materials in public libraries*, Monograph 18. Urbana, IL: University of Illinois Graduate School of Library and Information Science.

The usefulness of fill rates: Research and debate. (1988). *Public Libraries, 27*, 15–32.

Van House, Nancy. (1983). Output measures: Some lessons from Baltimore County public library. *Public Libraries, 24*, 102–105.

Van House, Nancy, Lynch, Mary Jo, McClure, Charles R., & Zweizig, Douglas L. (1987). *Output measures for public libraries* (2nd ed.). Chicago: American Library Association.

Zweizig, Douglas, & Rodger, Eleanor Jo. (1982). *Output measures for public libraries*. Chicago: American Library Association.

2

Reflections on Performance Measures Fifteen Years Later

Ellen Altman

Graduate Library School
University of Arizona
Tucson, AZ

ASSESSING IMPACT

Most things are easier said than done, more easily written about than implemented. That certainly has been the case with performance measures for public libraries. The two monographs generated by the "Measurement of the Effectiveness of Public Library Service" study on which Ernest DeProspo, Kenneth Beasley and I worked in the early 1970s—*Performance Measures for Public Libraries* (1973) and with Phillip M. Clark and Ellen Connor Clark, *A Data-Gathering and Instructional Manual for Performance Measures in Public Libraries* (Altman, DeProspo, Clark, & Clark, 1976)—are among the most widely cited library-related publications of the 1970s. Interest in the performance measures monographs as measured by continuing references to them has lasted well into the 1980s as shown on Table 2.1 Citations to "Performance Measures" Monographs by Year.

I recently finished an analysis of the impact of research and demonstration projects awarded under Title II-B of the Higher Education Act of 1965 (Altman & Antieau, 1988). Impact was measured by the number of citations to those projects listed in *Social Science Citation Index* from 1965 to August 1987. The citations referred to a sample of 163 (52%) of the 312 research and demonstration projects funded by the United States Office/Department of Education's Office of Libraries and Learning Resources. The sample also included books and journal articles produced or spun off from those projects.

It was both gratifying and slightly embarrassing to discover that the two monographs emanating from the "Measurement of the Effectiveness of Public Library Service" study received twice as many citations as any other research and development project analyzed. At last count, excluding book reviews, *Performance Measures* had been cited

Table 2.1. Citations to "Performance Measures" Monographs by Year

Year	73	74	75	76	77	78	79	80	81	82	83	84	85	86	87
Cited	2	6	7	12	13	28	12	17	10	7	19	5	4	4	6

in 26 monographs and 93 times in serials and the *Instructional Manual* in 9 and 24, respectively. It is quite likely that some references remain undetected since citations in monographs are spottily indexed and thus difficult to track down.

The span of topics covered by writers citing these works has been surprisingly broad, ranging over papers on planning, collection development, administration, information science, public services, user studies, and standards development. The diversity of journals in which reference has been made to performance measures is also surprising. They include *The Annual Review of Information Science and Technology, Law Library Journal, Journal of Academic Librarianship, Library Resources and Technical Services, JASIS, College and Research Libraries, Library Quarterly, Special Libraries, Government Publications Review, Serials Librarian, Medical Library Association Bulletin,* and *Catholic Library World,* as well as publications devoted to public libraries and/or research where citations would be normally expected.

Citations have also appeared in journals published outside the United States such as *UNESCO Bulletin for Libraries, Ontario Library Review, Canadian Library Journal, Information Processing and Management, Journal of Documentation, Library and Information Science* (Japan). Even journals outside librarianship have published papers containing citations to performance measures. These include *Land Economics, Industrial and Labor Relations Review,* and *Socio-Economic Planning Sciences.*

Although the first published report of the study, *Performance Measures for Public Libraries,* received a number of generally favorable reviews and generated subsequent invitations for us to speak at a number of local, state, and national library association meetings and even an ALA preconference, initial interest on the part of the audience far exceeded action to implement the measures proposed in the study.

There were libraries who used the manual and attempted the measures on their own. Librarians from some of these were thought- and sufficiently interested to write us with questions and comments about their experiences. Two articles (Schrader, 1980; Fairfield & Rowland, 1978) were published describing some metropolitan Toronto libraries' experiences and their reactions to the measures. After De-Prospo's visit to Australia, the Library Council of Victoria (Ramsden, 1978) published an account of the use of the measures in Melbourne libraries.

Support on a fairly large scale came from North Suburban Library System outside Chicago, the Mississippi Department of Public Library Development, and the Office of Library Development, and Services for the state of Minnesota, all of whom invited us to conduct workshops for their constituents. On an even larger scale the state libraries of Illinois and New Jersey funded studies to test performance measures in their states. But all of these attempts were essentially one-shot efforts. We had hopes that performance measures would evolve into a systematic process which would, if not replace the traditional, descriptive library statistics, at least enhance them.

A PARTICIPANT'S REFLECTIONS

Reflecting back on experiences, I have concluded some rather important things about applied research. First, it is difficult to breach the gulf between research and practice, especially when there is no guaranteed payoff to practitioners, such as the development of a product or a process to increase productivity or profit; and second, the time lag between the development of an idea and its adoption by the field is a long one—a fact documented in other professional disciplines as well. Because libraries have no competitors in the same sense that businesses do, and because there is no balance sheet to indicate how well the organization is doing, there is little or no pressure to change.

Further reflection prompts me to conclude that the limited impact of the performance measures, as evidenced by the relative few libraries which adopted the methods, was partly, perhaps mostly, the fault of the developers of the measures. Although we consciously set out to develop measures which were easy and straightforward enough to be implemented by the library's own staff, I believe we seriously underestimated:

1. The staff time required to collect some of the information.
2. Most library administrators' reluctance to commit so much time.

We also greatly overestimated staff ability to tabulate and analyze the data.

A *Data-Gathering and Instructional Manual for Performance Measures for Public Libraries* was published in 1976. At that time few public libraries had either the staff expertise or computer resources to make tabulation fast and easy. Having to make so many tabulations by hand or having to negotiate the programming and interface problems of dealing with the city or county computer department to process the data seemed a horrendous task for most librarians, and indeed it usually was. The microcomputer and spreadsheet programs which are now so readily available and user-friendly and which compile and analyze such data so easily were unknown to us and to most librarians at that time. Today, one can buy a template program to rapidly crunch the numbers for *Output Measures for Public Libraries.* Clarion University (Vavrek, 1984) can provide a software example.

With the rapid development of library software and the increasing competition as more vendors enter the market, I suspect that within a few years programs will be developed which will monitor keyboarded queries for materials not owned by the library, those already in circulation and the number of queries per subject heading. Daily, weekly, monthly, and yearly summaries of user's hits and misses in finding materials could be provided. By utilizing computers, *getting* such data is easy. *Using* the information is something else.

THE MAJOR PROBLEM

The most formidable problem to the practitioner was interpreting the results. Historically, libraries had been conditioned to compare their "goodness" (as Michael K. Buckland calls it) against American Library Association-endorsed standards for public libraries or against descriptive statistics for like-sized libraries published by their state libraries or the federal government (National Center for Education Statistics, 1986). The inference was that if one's library exceeded similarly sized libraries in the data categories reported, then the library's goodness was assured. Because of this prior and longstanding conditioning, practitioners wanted to use the performance measures data in the same way. At meetings at which we spoke, we were frequently asked about comparing the data to findings for other libraries. Our inability and *unwillingness* to make such comparisons caused practitioners a certain amount of frustration and dismay.

THE DIFFICULTY WITH COMPARISONS AND OUR STANCE ON PERSPECTIVES

One reason for our seeming uncooperativeness was that the sample used in the 1973 initial report was so small in each of the three size breakdowns that we knew the figures could not reliably reflect expected probability values for each of the measures. The other reason that comparisons could not be made was more complicated. The project team was philosophically opposed to the practice of standard comparisons because of the arbitrary way in which they were set and the general lack of care used in making the comparisons. Had we taken it upon ourselves to pronounce that certain numbers were "good" or "bad," we, too, would have been rightly accused of being arbitrary. We felt that taken as a whole, the measurement process allowed administrators and senior staff to analyze the measures in terms of the library as a system—to evaluate which parts were working well in terms of what *they* wanted to accomplish in *their* libraries and which needed to be improved.

Practitioners, on the other hand, seemed to want a score that would tell them if results for each measure were good or bad. Because the research was an exploratory study, there was no basis on which to judge whether findings were good or bad. Nor could we at that time measure improvements in scores since that would have required time-line data gathered over some years. Also, it seemed unrealistic to expect a similar range of goodness or badness because of the wide size ranges encompassed within the arbitrary classification of small, medium, and large libraries. Intuitively, one might expect that performance would be better in large, well-funded organizations. The study team felt strongly, however, that each library staff should decide for themselves whether the findings for that library were acceptable in terms of performance expectations. The project team which developed the *Output Measures* faced the same problems, since the profession has no widely accepted definitions of goodness. Until these are established, all such measurement/comparison efforts are groping in the dark.

CHANGE AGENTS' DILEMMA

We found that changing the conditioning, attitudes, and ways of practicing is a difficult process which takes a long time to affect people removed from researchers in time and space, especially when they are busy with other pressing daily concerns—like providing library services. Although we were well aware that numerical illiteracy or, at least, math anxiety, was widespread in the profession, we naively assumed that the calculations in the measurement process were so simple as to be readily comprehended by anyone who read the publications. And so the project team failed to understand just how difficult and complicated the process of educating the busy and distant practitioner would be. In fact, this was the area that we overlooked, much to the detriment of widespread acceptance of the measures. I have been asked if librarians entering the profession since our study are more numerically literate. I'd have to say yes and no. Those who have learned how to manipulate data using spreadsheet programs will not feel overwhelmed by tabulating a lot of data. On the other hand, my experience in trying to make students understand that only grade school arithmetic is required to put a relatively simple library budget together discourages me and leads me to believe the problem persists.

FOR CHANGE TO "TAKE"

Organizations adopt products or processes only when they believe it is in their benefit to do so or when mandated by higher administration. Higher administration gave no such mandate to implement performance measures as defined in this study nor did state libraries or the National Center for Education Statistics. The obvious benefit in adopting performance measures was to demonstrate to funders and the community how "good" were the services provided by the libraries. Since the methodology developed provided no "goodness" score, however, the payoff to the libraries seemed nonexistent or unclear. According to Mary Jo Lynch, director of the ALA Office for Research, some 15 states have now agreed informally to request some of the output measures—the number of reference transactions, number of library visits, and program attendance—on future annual reports sent to public libraries within their states. But the Center for Educational Statistics prefers to continue to collect only descriptive data. So, the likelihood that output measures will become a widely used, standard reporting method appears doubtful.

PERHAPS IT WAS THE NAME!

I harbor an unproven assumption that the name we chose—performance measures—might have given the impression that the payoff was negative. The term *performance* has primarily been used in the evaluation of personnel. Although we tried to convey the message that this project was not intended to evaluate individual staff, the suspicions that the data might be used in that way were difficult to overcome. The project team that developed the Output Measures may have intuitively sensed those suspicions and wisely chose a less pejorative term for their measures.

Because the Office for Libraries and Learning Resources declined to fund the second phase of the "Measurement of the Effectiveness of Public Library Service" study which would have included on-site visits to the demonstration libraries to determine to what extent the measurement indicators coincided with professional judgment about the effectiveness of service and a microanalysis of the data collected by the demonstration libraries, the project team was forced to disband. We did continue promoting the project through speaking engagements, securing funds to implement the study in a number of libraries in New Jersey, and finally published the *Instruction Manual* in 1976. Although we stopped our activities on measurement in 1976, we were pleased that other researchers such as Paul Kantor and the staff at King Research—Palmour, Zweizig, and Rodger—continued to explore new measures and to refine those used in our project.

TIME AND CHANGE

To paraphrase Sir Francis Bacon, "Time is the greatest innovator." In the 15 or so years that have passed since we started working on performance measures, certain changes have occurred which have made the profession more receptive to the idea of measuring library services. A frequent objection voiced to us in the early 1970s was that it was impossible to measure the quality of service—the pleasure a child derived from a story hour, or the insight one got from reading a book, or the usefulness of an accurate answer to a reference question. Today, I think librarians are more willing to understand that if there are no story hours, if the desired book cannot be procured, or if the correct answer cannot be provided, then quality is affected. In other words, quantifiable activities or objects must first be provided before quality can be inferred.

Another change in attitude has been the willingness to accept sampling in lieu of counting the universe of objects and activities found in libraries. All subsequent "measurement studies" have used samples.

A far more significant factor has been the willingness to abandon a single set of public library standards as the *sine qua non* of "goodness." By doing so, the Public Library Association (1979), in the *Public Library Mission Statement and Its Imperatives for Service,* has fostered acceptance of the idea that libraries should plan and evaluate service programs "appropriate to the needs of a specific community," thus implying that libraries can be different and good at the same time. Even more important, the idea of comparisons among libraries as a standard of quality has been diluted.

Most important of all has been PLA's shift from the historical precedent of counting inputs—volumes, budget, staff, which indicate only the capacity to perform rather than actual performance, to an emphasis on the measurement of outputs. This shift represents a fundamental turn from focusing primarily on institutional resources to a concern for users and their individual needs. All in all, I think Ernie would be pleased.

REFERENCES

Altman, Ellen, De Prospo, Ernest R., Clark, Philip M., & Clark, Ellen Connor. (1976). *A data-gathering and instructional manual for performance measures in public libraries.* Chicago: Celadon Press.

Altman, Ellen, & Antieau, Kim. (1988). Dissemination and impact of U. S. Department of Education's library research and demonstration projects: A citation analysis. *Government Information Quarterly, 5,* 45–56.

DeProspo, Ernest R., Beasley, Kenneth E., & Altman, Ellen. (1973). *Performance measures for public libraries.* Chicago: Public Library Association, American Library Association.

Fairfield, J., & Rowland, Betty. (1978). Measuring library performance: The experience of four Ontario public libraries. *Ontario Library Review, 62,* 9–16.

National Center for Education Statistics. (1986). *Survey of public libraries: 1981–82.* Chicago: Public Library Association.

Public Library Association. (1979). *Public library mission statement and its imperatives for service.* Chicago: The Public Library Association.

Ramsden, M. J. (1978). *Performance measurement of some Melbourne public libraries: A report to the Library Council of Victoria.* Melbourne: Library council of Victoria.

Schrader, Alvin M. (1980). Performance measures for public libraries: Refinements in methodology and reporting. *Library Research, 2,* 129–55.

Vavrek, Bernard. (1984). *Outputm* [diskette]. Clarion: Clarion State University.

3
Integrating Performance Measures into the Planning Process: Moving Toward Decision Support Systems

Charles R. McClure

School of Information Studies
Syracuse University

INTRODUCTION

Since the introduction of *Performance Measures for Public Libraries* (DeProspo et al., 1973), considerable attention has been given to the evaluation of library services through the use of performance measures. In addition, some attention has been given to the development and implementation of library planning processes. However, there appears to be a "failure to communicate" the importance of integrating evaluation concepts and performance measures into a broader administrative context related to decision making and planning.

Although planning includes numerous activities, traditionally, it has been defined as dealing with these primary areas:

* Assessing the library and information needs of the library's community
* Developing written mission statements and goals/objectives
* Designing programs and activities to accomplish the objectives
* Evaluating the success of these activities.

Planning is based on the assumption that change is both natural and necessary; that there is consistent and ongoing administrative support for the planning process; that library staff can, in fact, change and improve library services; and that the quality of library services can be measured.

The term *performance measure,* which is a broader and more generic term than output measures, refers to any type of quantitative measure that assesses the efficiency (allocation of resources) or effectiveness (accomplishment of objectives) of the library. An output measure, a type of performance measure, concentrates on the effectiveness or quality of the services or products which the library offers its clientele.

Performance measures are primarily supportive in the sense that they can provide indicators to assess the degree of change that has occurred as a result of the planning process. They are self-diagnostic tools that can enable librarians (and others) to evaluate the degree to which objectives are accomplished and thus provide the feedback for the library's planning activities by (a) documenting improvements in the effectiveness and efficiency of library activities, and (b) suggesting areas where library services can be improved. But such "feedback" needs to be organized to support decision making.

Decision support systems (DSS) are computer-based information systems that assist decision makers in resolving semistructured problems—problems with considerable ambiguity, for example. Typically, the DSS allows the decision maker to format and structure the information in such a way that it can be adapted to the problem solving and cognitive styles of the individual rather than the other way around. According to Young (1984), "A DSS does not impose a decision-making process on the user, but rather provides the decision maker with a set of capabilities that can be applied . . . in a form that fits his or her cognitive style" (p. 58).

A DSS assumes that the organization engages in a rational decision-decision-making process: that it has a specific objective or problem to be resolved, compares at least two different alternative solutions, and includes empirical data to assist in the decision-making process. In short, a librarian wishing to use a DSS must be knowledgeable about computer-based information systems, have effective decision-making procedures, and provide supportive management styles and organizational climates.

But what are the specific relationships between planning, performance measures, and a DSS, and how can libraries integrate them effectively into an overall administrative strategy? To answer this question, this chapter will provide a brief historical perspective on the development of library planning, performance measures, and DSS. Next, the importance of DSS as an administrative tool will be stressed. The chapter will conclude by suggesting that DSS must be integrated—both conceptually and practically—with planning approaches and the use of performance measures.

This chapter is not intended to be either a tutorial on how to plan, how to use performance measures, or how to establish a library DSS. It assumes that the reader has some basic familiarity with these processes as well as a basic knowledge of library administration. Further,

Figure 3.1.   Integrating Planning and Performance Measure Components with Decision Support Systems

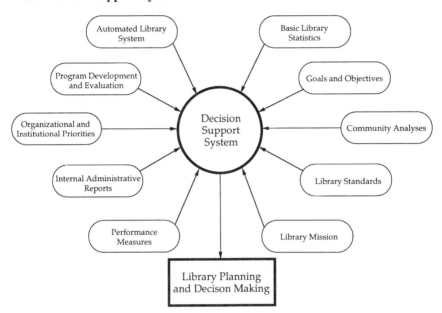

it will not provide a review of the literature on library planning, performance measures, or DSS. It will, however, argue that the three processes can be better integrated and, indeed, must be better integrated if planning approaches and use of performance measures are to significantly affect overall library organizational effectiveness.

Currently, various activities typically associated with planning and evaluation are poorly integrated into library decision making. Indeed, as suggested in Figure 3.1, a range of factors and activities combine for a successful DSS. However, these activities may be done in isolation from each other. For instance:

- Community analysis data may not be transformed into performance measures.
- Goals and objectives may not be established for the library or evaluated on a regular planning cycle.
- Data from existing library activities and operations, such as an automated circulation system, may be excluded from the needs assessment process.
- The evaluation of organization programs is not conducted in connection with existing goals and objectives.
- Planning may be done without a needs assessment process.

The isolation of the various activities related to planning and evaluation limits their usefulness. Decision support systems are necessary to link these activities together and provide a mechanism that assists librarians to translate the planning and evaluation activities into decisions and action. Figure 3.1 displays these activities.

Background

Although there was interest in the development of various types of quantitative measures of library performance prior to the early 1970s, the work by DeProspo, Altman, and Beasley (1973) stands as a benchmark event. This publication, *Performance Measures for Public Libraries*, has significance because:

- It advocated a program of activities related to the development and use of performance measures.
- It proposed a methodology that allowed one library to compare its performance on a range of measures against that of similar libraries.
- It placed emphasis on developing measures that examined both the use of library resources and the provision of library services.
- It advocated a process that appeared to be doable by the professional community and had high credibility.

Equally as important, the DeProspo study encouraged the development of an *attitude* on the part of librarians—an attitude prompting them to want to engage in a process that generates ongoing evaluative data about the performance of the library.

At the time, a concern of DeProspo was the failure of *Performance Measures* to discuss the use of performance measures within a context of planning. To that end, DeProspo worked with the College Entrance Examination Board (DeProspo, 1973) and developed a number of mimeograph manuals related to program planning and evaluation, or PP&E as he referred to it. Based, in part, on the CIPP (Context, Input, Process, Product) model developed at Ohio State University, the manuals were intended to:

- Assist librarians develop action programs which will enable the library to provide services effectively and efficiently.
- Provide a "no nonsense," straight forward approach to incorporate planning with evaluation.

In DeProspo's view, the linking of planning and evaluation was a key element for increasing library effectiveness. The overall project was never completed, and *Performance Measures for Public Libraries* did not reflect his view that the evaluation component of planning could, in fact, be composed of performance measures. Such an idea was one heard frequently in the doctoral seminars and small group discussions at Rutgers.

The next large-scale effort in the area of library planning came as a result of the Management Review and Analysis Program (MRAP) from the Association of Research Libraries, Office of Management Studies (Webster, 1974). While some debate continues on whether MRAP was a planning process or a self-review process, it had wide impact on academic libraries in the mid- to late-1970s (Johnson & Mann, 1980). The emphasis of the program, however, was on data collection and needs assessment. Specific strategies for analyzing the descriptive data either in terms of performance measures or of implementing change through a formalized planning process were not clear.

A SHARPER FOCUS ON PLANNING

Meanwhile, the Public Library Association had obtained funding for a project in the area of planning and evaluation which resulted in *A Planning Process for Public Libraries* (Palmour et al., 1980). Produced by King Research, Inc., the *Planning Process for Public Libraries* was introduced in the early 1980s as a manual for public library planning. Strangely, however, the specific links between the *Planning Process for Public Libraries* and *Performance Measures for Public Libraries* were not made explicit.

Interestingly both the MRAP program, developed primarily for academic librarians, and *Planning Process for Public Libraries* have been criticized for similar reasons; they:

- Place too much emphasis on needs assessment and data collection.
- Fail to incorporate performance measures as part of the evaluation process.
- Give limited attention to the development of library missions, goals, and objectives.
- Provide inadequate procedures for data analysis, reporting, and presentation strategies.

Despite these criticisms it should be noted that as of 1980 the three primary planning and evaluation manuals were *Performance Measures for Public Libraries*, the Management Review and Analysis Program, and *A Planning Process for Public Libraries*.

In the late 1970s interest continued to mount in performance measures and in procedures for their collection and analysis. The Public Library Association responded with *Output Measures for Public Libraries* (Zweizig & Rodger, 1982). The manual described 12 output measures for use in a public library context. The procedures for collecting the data were straightforward, and "level two" measures (additional measures) were provided for those willing to tackle more sophisticated measures. The manual has had remarkable distribution and awareness in the public library community. However, the publication was not linked, procedurally, to previous efforts on the part of the Public Library Association in performance measures or planning development.

MIS AND DSS

Also during the early 1980s there was an increased interest in the development of management information systems (MIS) to support library decision making. Publications by Bommer and Chorba (1982) and later by Dowlin (1982) offered practical suggestions regarding the development of library systems for management information. The system in place at Pikes Peak Library District, Colorado Springs, appears to be one of the few working examples of a library-wide, integrated decision support system (Dowlin, 1984).

Library MIS and DSS, however, can best be described as theory in search of a practice. Reasons for the lack of development in library MIS and DSS can be linked to a number of factors (McClure, 1984):

- There have been few (if any) funded research and development programs for the design, implementation, and testing of library MIS and DSS.
- No practical, "how-to" manuals are available (such as *Output Measures for Public Libraries* for performance measures) for local library development of DSS.
- MIS and DSS do not have significant credibility as effective administrative tools in libraries.
- Many librarians operate under the misconception that an automated system, such as a circulation system, provides a decision support system.
- Many librarians lack the technical skills for the development of management information systems (regardless of the type).
- Many library management styles are not conducive to the development and use of MIS and DSS as an aid in planning and decision making (McClure & Samuels, 1985).

These and other factors have combined to significantly retard the development and use of MIS or DSS in the library administrative environment (Lynch, 1985), although at least one public library MIS has recently been implemented and described in the literature (McClure, Haggerty-Roach, Ruth, & England, 1989).

Despite the struggling attempts to implement DSS in the library environment, work continued on the development of performance measures and planning procedures. In the academic library setting, *Objective Performance Measures for Academic and Research Libraries* (Kantnor, 1984) appeared. This publication provided a sophisticated methodology to examine aspects of materials availability, analysis of patron activities, and delay analysis. In each of these areas, specific performance measures are described with procedures for data collection and analysis. Yet in this publication and in the 1985 appearance of *Performance Measurement for Public Services in Academic and Research Libraries* (Cronin, 1985), the use of measures is not clearly linked to a long-range planning process or integration into library decision making.

CONTINUED EFFORTS TO PROMOTE PLANNING

In addition, publications have appeared such as *Strategic Planning in ARL Libraries* (Association for Research Libraries, 1984) and the 1984 *Strategic Planning for Library Managers* (Riggs, 1984). The examples in the ARL publication, however, neither relate strategic planning to the use of performance measure nor describe the role of a DSS as an aid to the strategic planning process. *Strategic Planning for Library Managers* provides excellent coverage of planning basics, but gives only eight pages to the role of a management information system for strategic planning and does not mention the use of performance measures in strategic planning. Indeed, neither the DeProspo group's work on performance measures nor Zweizig's and Rodger's work on output measures is mentioned.

A number of state libraries are engaged in the development of planning and performance measures. In an attempt to promote state-wide library development, manuals are being developed in Oklahoma (Oklahoma Department of Libraries, 1982, 1985) and in the state of Utah (Utah Advisory Committee, 1986) that provide procedures for local library planning and integrating that planning into the use of performance measures as a means of ongoing evaluation and development of statewide public library standards. However, neither of these manuals assists the local libraries or the state library to organize, analyze, and integrate the management information collected for planning and performance measures into a decision support system.

AN IMPORTANT STEP TOWARD LINKING MEASUREMENT
AND PLANNING

Interest in the development of library performance measures and refinement of planning continues. A most significant event was the 1987 publication of *Planning & Role Setting for Public Libraries* (McClure, Owen, Zweizig, Lynch, & Van House, 1987) and *Output Measures for Public Libraries*, Second edition (Van House, Lynch, McClure, Zweizig, & Rodger, 1987). These manuals, published as a result of the Public Library Association sponsored Public Library Development Program, are a first and important attempt to link planning and performance measures. Equally important, they attempt to do so in a clear and easy-to-apply set of procedures.

With standardized collection and reporting of public library performance measures, efforts can be made to produce nationally comparable performance measure data. Such a listing appeared in *Statistical Report '88* (1988) which compiled a range of library statistical data (including performance measures) for some 400 public libraries.

Interest appears to be high within the library community to continue working toward improved procedures for collecting performance measures. The Public Library Association *Statistical Report* is intended to be an annual publication with additional libraries reporting each year. In addition, the Association of College and Research Libraries has contracted for the development, testing, and writing of a performance measures manual for academic libraries (Van House, Weil, & McClure, in press).

Curiously, national attention has yet to be given to questions such as: What will librarians do with all this performance measure data? What other types of management information should be collected and organized for decision making? How will the data be organized, maintained, analyzed, reported, and used in the decision-making process? Thus, as we refine our efforts to obtain library performance measure data, librarians must also consider how we will manage this data and how it can be best utilized to improve decision making.

Recently, questions have been raised regarding the quality of the data being produced by the various performance measures. One recent study (Van House, 1985) suggests that a number of the output measures related to availability of library materials are not valid because libraries do not collect data from large enough sample sizes. Another researcher (D'Elia, 1985) believes that much of the variance in performance measure data is simply the result of standard error. These and similar studies serve as important reminders that any performance measure data collection process must result in the gathering of reliable and valid data.

This brief background section has shown that in the development of three library administrative tools, planning, performance measures, and decision support systems are typically treated as isolates. All the various factors and activities shown on Figure 3.1 typically are *not* integrated in decision making. Attention must be given to the development of management tools that *integrate* the use of performance measures in planning. A decision support system serves as such a link to integrate the various planning and performance measure processes.

INFORMATION FOR DECISION SUPPORT SYSTEMS

Virtually every model of a planning process or of decision making involves a component where:

- The information needed is identified and procedures for its collection are developed.
- The information is checked for reliability and validity.
- The information is analyzed in terms of the decision objectives or the strategic plans.
- The information is presented in a report format that is intended to meet the cognitive style of the planners or decision makers.

Yet, in the typical library setting, more attention is given to *how* the data are to be collected than to *what* is to be done with the data and *which* decision situations they are intended to support.

A number of librarians find the data collection process too cumbersome, regardless of whether that data collection is for performance measures, user information, financial data, or whatever. Those that do engage in a formalized process of the collection of ongoing library management information such as that described by Brown (1982) typically fail to use that information as support for planning and decision making. Indeed, a broad perspective of the various information gathering techniques that have caught the attention of librarians, community analysis, performance measures, and zero-based budgeting, for example, suggests that library administrators (a) prefer not to have to engage in ongoing collection of management information; and (b) if engaged in the collection of management information, typically fail to integrate the information on a regular and ongoing basis into planning and decision making.

Among the reasons that the information collected as a result of community analysis, performance measurement process, or whatever, fails to be utilized for planning and decision making are:

- It is not clear what, if anything, can be done about whatever the data purport to show.
- The data are not trusted, or an error is found and is used to invalidate the entire report.
- The data do not clearly indicate if something is "good" or "bad"; there is no indication of the value of an activity (Is a title fill rate of 47% good or bad?).
- The data collectors are unable (lack the skills) to convince the administrators that the information means anything.
- The users of the management information are predisposed to what they believe (regardless of the data) and may have their own management information.
- The information cannot be compared across library departments on similar or equal units of measure (Shank, 1983).

In addition, there are organizational climate considerations that can effectively eliminate the integration of information into planning and decision making:

- Top administration management style does not support the use of organizational resources for managing information for planning and decision making.
- Library staff are not familiar with management uses of organizational information and see themselves as providers of information to clientele.
- Library staff lack the necessary technical skills to identify, obtain, analyze, and present information to support planning and decision making.

Further, a constant criticism with library planning approaches and uses of performance measures by librarians "in the trenches" is that having such information doesn't make any difference in what is actually done in the library (McClure, 1986). As a result of these and other organizational factors, when management information is collected (such as data for producing performance measures), it tends to be poorly integrated into the planning and decision-making processes of the library.

AN IMPORTANT DIFFERENCE TO OBSERVE AND CONSIDER

The difference between the collection of library-related information (information broadly describing library operations and activities) and strategic information must be stressed. Strategic information (Reinharth, Shapiro, & Kalliman, 1981) is that which is related to a specific decision situation and reduces the uncertainty state of the individual decision maker for semistructured and unstructured decision situations. Strategic information allows the planner or decision maker to ask "what if . . . " questions such as:

• If circulation increases by 15% how will the availability of library materials be affected?
• If the library increases the accuracy with which it answers reference questions, how much additional staff will be required?
• Will an increase of 150 serial subscriptions for science and technology increase the research productivity of the faculty in these areas?

By and large, however, the data that are collected for performance measures are not organized and analyzed in such a way that the staff can readily access the information, ask "what if . . . " questions, or make inferences on future activities in the library (McClure, Haggerty-Roach, Ruth & England, 1989).

MOVING TOWARD INTEGRATION

The primary purposes for planning and measuring performance are to improve the organizational effectiveness of the library (as defined by the library's goals and objectives) and to improve the degree to which the library meets and resolves the information needs of library clientele. Thus far, library planning and performance measurement have failed to fulfill their potential as effective administrative tools. One of the primary reasons for this failure is the lack of a conceptual framework that links strategic information to library decision makers and planners in a meaningful way.

Individual administrative strategies, such as planning, zero-based budgeting, applying performance measures, or whatever, must be integrated within the library through an information system, minimally, that:

• Regularly collects and analyzes organizational and environmental data related to the library.

- Is easily accessible to library staff throughout the library and is "user friendly."
- Allows the decision makers and planners to ask "what if . . . " questions and identify alternate scenarios as a result of making one decision rather than another.
- Provides for comparable units of measure both within and across libraries.
- Produces information in multiple formats (graphic, tabular, report, etc.) and matches the presentation format to the cognitive styles of various users.

Until such decision support systems are in place, libraries engaged in formalized planning approaches and the use of performance measures are likely to have:

- Fragmented sets of data collected by different persons, under different definitions, which cannot be analyzed over time.
- Data located in different areas of the library but one department may be unaware of data collected by other departments.
- Limited ability to make *organizational-wide* decisions that are based on empirical evidence.
- Uncoordinated plans and strategies across the library.
- Limited knowledge about the impact of allocating one type of library resource on other resources.

Worse, engaging in planning and the use of performance measures without adequate information system support may result in a hardening of staff attitude that "planning and data collection to compute performance measures really doesn't make any difference anyway, so why bother?"

Clearly, the collection of performance measure statistics is not the same as having an information system that provides direct decision support. Nonetheless, standard library statistics can be an integral part of a decision support system (Runyon, 1981). The issue to be resolved is the degree to which management information can be integrated into the planning and decision making process. The mentality for collection of library statistics is not the same as the administrative mentality for the collection of data as *part* of a decision support system.

Planning approaches must be *dynamic* processes that encourage change to occur—not only in the library organization, but within the planning process itself. Recent management literature has noted that much of the strategic planning approaches are "portfolio-based"—

based on environmental determinism and hierarchical structure, focused on control, and encourage a competitive organizational culture. Developing planning approaches, described as "strategic self-renewal" are adaptive, based on strategic choices, encourage administrative autonomy and an organizational culture of collaborativeness (Chakravarthy, 1984). A critical ingredient for organizations wishing to move from "portfolio" to "strategic self-renewal" planning approaches is open access to a broad range of management information through decision support systems.

Perhaps one of the difficulties is the use of the term DSS. Such systems do not have to be large, mainframe computer-driven information systems. Indeed, there is much potential for the development of microcomputer-based library decision support systems with the availability of easy-to-use software such as data base managers and spreadsheets (Clark, 1985; Clark, 1989; Hernon & McClure, 1986). Since many libraries now have access to or own a microcomputer, they can develop basic decision support systems, link them through local area networks (LANS) throughout the library system, and make the information available to all staff members engaged in planning and decision making.

With such systems in place, decision makers can relate performance measure data to the degree with which specific objectives were accomplished, compare performance measure data across departments and libraries, develop predictive models describing relationships between the various performance measures, and find additional decision-making applications for the data. Currently, the performance measure data (that was collected so painstakingly) appears to some as a poor investment because of limited payoffs in terms of enhanced decision making. The difficulty is not with the performance measures or the planning approaches, the problem lies in our inability to effectively use and manipulate the data!

Librarians must be concerned about developing useful and powerful techniques of measurement and counting which, sadly, become ends unto themselves. During doctoral seminars, DeProspo was fond of referring to the "mystique of quantity." Briefly, the mystique is the failure to recognize the instrumentality of measurement, "which responds to numbers as though they were repositories of occult powers" (Kaplan, 1964, p. 172).

Measurement and evaluation are only means to a larger end of increased overall library effectiveness. As DeProspo (1982) wrote, "measurement is dependent on how well that thing to be measured is conceptualized. The poorer the conceptualization, the poorer the measure and consequently less effective and efficient the PP&E [Program Planning & Evaluation] endeavor." Currently, our ability to use planning and performance measures effectively is limited by our conceptual ability to integrate decision support systems into these processes. Once such integration occurs, libraries will be better able to make use of performance measure data and the various planning approaches that are being developed.

REFERENCES

Association of Research Libraries. (1984). *Strategic planning in ARL Libraries* [Spec Kit no. 108]. Washington, DC: Association of Research Libraries.

Bommer, Michael R. W., & Chorba, Ronald W. (1982). *Decision making for library management*. White Plains, NY: Knowledge Industry Publications.

Brown, Maryann Kevin. (1982). Information for planning. In C. R. McClure (Ed.), *Planning for library services: A guide to utilizing planning methods for library management* (pp. 187–216). New York: Haworth Press.

Chakravarthy, Balajii S. (1984). Strategic self-renewal: A planning framework for today. *Academy of Management Review, 9,* 536–547.

Clark, Philip M. (1989). Developing A Decision Support System: The Software and Hardware Tools. *Library Administration & Management, 3,* 184–191.

Clark, Philip M. (1985). *Microcomputer spreadsheet models for libraries: Preparing documents, budgets and statistical reports*. Chicago: American Library Association.

Cronin, Mary J. (1985). *Performance measurement for public services in academic and research libraries*. Washington, DC: Association of Research Libraries.

D'Elia, George. (1985). Materials availability fill rates—Useful measures of library performance? *Public Libraries, 24,* 106–110.

DeProspo, Ernest R. (1973). *A program planning and evaluation training manual*. New York: College Entrance Examination Board.

DeProspo, Ernest R., Altman, Ellen, & Beasley, Kenneth E. (1973). *Performance measures for public libraries*. Chicago: American Library Association.

DeProspo, Ernest R. (1982). The evaluation component of planning. In C. R. McClure (Ed.), *Planning for library services: A guide to utilizing planning methods for library management* (pp. 159–172). New York: Hayworth Press.

Dowlin, Kenneth E. (1982). The use of standard statistics in an online library management system. *Public Library Quarterly, 3,* 37–46.

Dowlin, Kenneth E. (1984). *The electronic library*. New York: Neal-Schuman.

Hernon, Peter, & McClure, Charles R. (Eds.). (1986). *Microcomputers for library decision making: Issues, trends, and applications*. Norwood, NJ: Ablex.

Johnson, Edward R., & Mann, Stuart H. (1980). *Organization development for academic libraries*. Westport, CT: Greenwood Press.

Kantor, Paul. (1984). *Objective performance measures for academic and research libraries*. Washington, DC: Association of Research Libraries.

Kaplan, Abraham. (1964). *The conduct of inquiry: Methodology for behavioral sciences*. Scranton, PA: Chandler Publishing.

Lynch, Mary Jo. (1985). Information technology, library management, and OCLC. *Information Technology and Libraries, 4,* 122–129.

McClure, Charles R. (1984). Management information for library decision making. In W. Simonton (Ed.), *Advances in librarianship* (Vol 13, pp. 1–47). New York: Academic Press.

McClure, Charles R. (1986). A view from the trenches: Costing and performance measures for academic library public services. *College & Research Libraries, 47,* 323–336.

McClure, Charles R., Haggerty-Roach, Liz, Ruth, Lindsay, & England, Pat. (1989). Design of a Public Library Management Information System: A Status Report. *Library Administration & Management, 3,* 192–198.

McClure, Charles R., Owen, Amy, Zweizig, Douglas L., Lynch, Mary Jo, & Van House, Nancy A. (1987). *Planning & role setting for public libraries*. Chicago: American Library Association.

McClure, Charles R., & Samuels, Alan R. (1985). Factors affecting the use of information for academic library decision making. *College and Research Libraries, 46,* 483–498.

Oklahoma Department of Libraries. (1982). *Performance measures for Oklahoma public libraries*. Oklahoma City, OK: Oklahoma Department of Libraries.

Oklahoma Department of Libraries. (1985). *Levels of library development: Reimaging the realm of the possible*. Oklahoma City, OK: Oklahoma Department of Libraries.

Palmour, Vernon E., Bellasai, Marcia C., & DeWath, Nancy. (1980). *A planning process for public libraries*. Chicago: American Library Association.

Reinharth, Leon, Shapiro, H. Jack, & Kalliman, Ernest A. (1981). *The practice of planning: Strategic, administrative, and operational*. New York: Van Nostrand Reinhold, Co.

Riggs, Donald E. (1984). *Strategic planning for library managers*. Phoenix: Oryx Press.

Runyon, R. S. (1981). Towards the development of a library management information system. *College and Research Libraries, 42,* 539–548.

Shank, Russell. (1983). Management, information and the organization: Homily from the experience of the data rich but information poor. In F. Wilfrid Lancaster (Ed.), *Library automation as a source of management information* (pp. 2–9). Champaign-Urbana: University of Illinois, Graduate School of Library and Information Science.

Statistical Report '88: PLDS, Public Library Data Service. (1988). Chicago: American Library Association.

Utah Advisory Committee. (1986). *Project upgrade: Planning, evaluating and measuring for public library excellence*. Salt Lake City: Utah State Library.

Van House, Nancy A., Lynch, Mary Jo, McClure, Charles R., Zweizig, Douglas L., & Rodger, Eleanor Jo. (1987). *Output measures for public libraries* (2nd ed.). Chicago: American Library Association.

Van House, Nancy A., Weil, Beth, McClure, Charles R. *Measuring Academic Library Performance: A Practical Approach*. (in press). Chicago: American Library Association.

Van House, Nancy A. (1985). Output measures: Some lessons from Baltimore county public library. *Public Libraries, 24*, 102–105.

Webster, Duane. (1974). The management review and analysis program. *College and Research Libraries, 35*, 114–125.

Young, Lawrence F. (1984). A corporate strategy for decision support systems. *Journal of Information Systems Management, 1*, 58.

Zweizig, Douglas, & Rodger, Eleanor Jo. (1982). *Output measures for public libraries*. Chicago: American Library Association.

4
Aspects of Validity in Unobtrusive Studies

Terence Crowley

Division of Library and Information Science
San Jose State University

INTRODUCTION

People solve problems in a variety of ways. Those who seek and obtain information for use in problem solving find that information comes primarily from interpersonal sources: close relatives and friends, professional colleagues, and community leaders. For some, getting materials and information services from a library is a means to solving problems. These patrons of libraries often seek information by asking questions either about the information or about how to use the books and other library materials in which they believe the information can be found. The examples of this kind of library use range from children asking about pet care to independent businessmen doing market research, from high school students researching term paper themes to senior citizens needing referral to social services. These simple examples illustrate the beginning of the complexity of library reference work, in which people of different ages ask questions of different kinds.

In addition to the variety of questions, there are varying levels of sophistication, of reading ability, and of time demands by the public. The librarians and other staff members who assist the public vary in their subject knowledge, motivation, and skill. The research on this complex of behaviors which go into library reference work is not very advanced; we have not generally begun to build on what we do know in order to improve the service. But some cumulative progress has been made in one research area: measuring some aspects of reference service which results in short, factual answers to unambiguous questions. Although it is a small part of reference work, few would deny that this service is important, or that nearly all libraries provide this kind of service. Perhaps there is a risk of confusing the performance in this narrow area with the larger service of which it is but a part (Childers, 1987).

BACKGROUND

The progress made in research into question-answering ability has been recounted recently (Crowley, 1985). For over 5,700 scored observations of questions asked unobtrusively in academic and public libraries the percentage of correct answers ranged from 37 to 80, with an average in the mid-50s.

Since that synthesis, two leading researchers have published the results of additional major studies (Hernon & McClure, 1987) in which they tested academic and public libraries; for 390 questions relating to government documents the overall success rate was 61.8 percent. In smaller local studies (Rodger & Goodwin, 1987; Hansel, 1986), the results have been similar, including one in which the questions were asked in law libraries (Way, 1987).

But there have also been objections and reactions to unobtrusive reference studies. Some researchers believe that we no longer need them because they have become redundant. Two recently published dissertations suggest that there is little difference in the results of questioning reference librarians obtrusively or unobtrusively (Benham & Powell, 1987). A Canadian critic abjures the context-free questions used and implicitly questions their validity. Rejecting the "paradigm of information as commodity," Ross argues that "because these contrived questions truly are decontextualized (no real person ever asked them)," they are an inappropriate model for "thinking about information" (Ross, 1986, p. 21).

In some ways, we seem to have reached a plateau on which future studies may test different types of questions, perhaps in different libraries, without questioning the validity of the basic approach.

UNOBTRUSIVE STUDIES

In unobtrusive reference studies, researchers are trying to judge the service which provides short, factual answers to unambiguous questions. They are trying to estimate the likelihood of an adult's receiving an accurate answer to just one of the many kinds of questions asked at libraries. By concentrating on this relatively easy-to-measure service, researchers are excluding many important elements of reference work, such as bibliographic instruction, online searching, answering research questions, reference material selection, and de-selection. Some researchers additionally seek to determine if reference accuracy is related to some other measure of library activity, for example, budget, staff experience and training, or collection size. These are questions which have some bearing on the quality of service, however obliquely or indirectly.

The purpose of this chapter is to examine some aspects of the validity of unobtrusive research in reference evaluation.

VALIDITY

As every graduate student in a research methods course soon learns, validity is a key element in research. If the student investigator is to satisfy the funders and consumers of research, she must persuade readers of the strength of her arguments. The original meaning of validity was related to the idea of strength of argument, essentially a rhetorical concept. Today, many researchers use the common sense definition that validity refers to the idea of measuring what you intend to measure. When some factor other than the one intended to be measured intervenes, the measure, and to some extent the research, loses validity. For example, public opinion pollsters attempt to determine people's opinion on a topic but actually may measure respondent's politeness. Also, or instead, the sources of invalidity of measures are many, and most are not easy to identify. But once these sources of invalidity become known, researchers can attempt to control for them or to measure in other ways which avoid the identified validity problem.

Unobtrusive research in reference work came about in part because of questions about the validity of two measures of reference accuracy: reference librarians' self-reports and patron responses to survey questionnaires. The very high scores from these measures did not agree with the much lower scores obtained experimentally in situations which avoided the systematic bias of self-reporting and survey research. Thus the earlier measures lost their validity.

The validity of unobtrusive studies rests in large part on the choice of questions which are used to measure the service. In some studies the questions are "made up"; in others they are taken exclusively from lists of questions which have been asked at libraries; in some studies, there is a mixture. As successive studies became more sophisticated, panels of experienced reference librarians have been called on to judge the questions for representativeness, difficulty, and other factors.

QUESTIONS

In educational testing situations, care is taken to insure that the questions fairly represent the material which is the subject of the test. But since libraries typically put no boundaries on the questions which they will attempt, all questions become eligible. The issue then becomes one of representativeness.

Do the questions asked at the tested libraries represent the universe of questions which have or will be asked at those particular libraries? This is perhaps the most significant hidden variable in unobtrusive measures. No study has ever asserted that the questions used do in fact represent the universe of questions which are peculiar to that particular library. Even in the narrow area of short-answer questions there are no assertions that the questions asked are representative either in kind or in relative proportion to the question experience of that library. Some studies spread their questions across categories of the Dewey Decimal System; others emphasize current affairs or government documents. In some studies questions have been asked, the answers to which are contained in sources which that library did not own. (Other studies were careful to determine which questions could in fact have been answered by sources within the library.) While the more recent studies, including Hernon and Mc-Clure, have used panels of experienced reference librarians to "certify" that the questions were reasonably representative of questions asked at the type of library targeted, these are judgments that have never been tested.

Most studies have used identical questions to be applied at each of the test sites. This is done so that the variable of the question is controlled by keeping it the same for each library; the measuring instrument does not change, except perhaps accidentally because of differences among proxies. In only one series of studies, those conducted at the University of Illinois Library Research Center, has there been an attempt to construct sets of equivalent questions so that while the questions at each library differ, a panel of judges certifies that they are comparable in difficulty. Here too, no claim was made concerning the representativeness of the questions for a particular library. In no study has there been an attempt to evaluate the judgment of the experts as they assessed the comparable or absolute difficulty of questions.

Nor has there been an attempt to choose questions that are representative in the sense that they are taken from lists of those asked at a particular library. And how might questions differ from library to library? We do not know, but the existence of local files of questions, of local indexes and reference sources (directories of local social service agencies, for example) suggests that there are differences.

On the other hand, there are factors which argue that questions asked at different libraries are similar if not the same: the so-called "core lists" of reference sources and the overlap between reference collections. Do libraries receive the same or similar questions? They must. Do they receive different and unique questions? They must. Do the questions differ over time? They must, as the fact of reference books going out of print attests. In sum, since librarians are presumably influenced by the experience they have answering reference questions in a particular library, questions designed to test their ability should ideally be drawn from the universe of questions asked at that library. The fact that this may be either impossible (because to do so would compromise the unobtrusive nature of the test and cause libraries to withdraw) or too costly (because researchers are always on tight budgets) should not blind us to this possible source of mismeasurement.

COMMUNITY DIFFERENCES

Should Questions and Libraries *Fit*?

Since librarians try hard to find out how communities differ, it seems that communities must differ in their composition in ways that affect library service. On the surface, this would seem obvious. Some members of a wealthy community are likely to be more interested in sailing and investments, some members of a less wealthy one in bowling and auto repair. Some people in agricultural communities have interests that some people in urban areas do not. We think these differences matter, but there is little research to substantiate the difference it makes to the reference librarians answering questions. Dervin's and Fraser's latest study (1985) suggests that the most significant factors in people's use of information are demonstrated in the way they conceptualize their progress towards making sense of their lives.

The way questions are asked is a part of the experience reference librarians have in a given community. Perhaps the grossest measure is that of language. It seems obvious that a set of English-language questions cannot be administered, with any expectation that the questions will receive representative answers, to a library serving a predominantly Spanish speaking community.

Lacking a comprehensive study which spells out how different community variables affect the mix of questions, we assume that it is legitimate to ask the same questions of different libraries. Only in the Library Research Study tests were different questions asked of different libraries, and there was no attempt reported to fit the various questions to the communities. It is likely that the questions which were applied were selected randomly from the pool judged to have been equal in difficulty.

The question of representativeness is complicated by the fact that few reference librarians will turn away a question which appears to be asked by a legitimate member of the library community unless it is in one of the taboo categories of medicine, law, or to a lesser extent, consumer evaluation. Therefore, any question applied unobtrusively from one who appears to be a "patron" is likely to evoke an attempt to answer it.

This kind of across-the-board questioning would seem to negate the possibility that a staff's experience in question answering is likely to affect its ability over time. Thus if Library A is used in a class assignment from elementary teacher Ms. Politics, who requires each student to write the names of the current presidential cabinet, then the reference librarians in A would seem more likely to be aware of changes in that cabinet than the librarians in a library which does not routinely answer such a question. If a university library has a librarian who routinely contacts a political science professor and helps her plan her methodology course around the use of specific reference sources, that librarian is likely to do better on questions emanating from the course than her colleague who has a different assignment. These are, of course, assumptions, and should be tested.

An Ideal Methodology?

Is there an ideal way to select questions for an unobtrusive study? Probably not if one is to be realistic and recognize the tradeoffs in expense required by a better system. Surely a better way of forming a list of questions would be to take them from the experience of the library being tested so that they were representative of the past universe of questions which had been asked.

If such a pool of questions representative of those asked at the target library were forthcoming, what other criteria might be used to insure an appropriate instrument? The judgment of a panel, used in many studies, can be brought to bear.

PANELS

Estimates of the difficulty of questions are perhaps the most used kinds of panel judgments. The panel is given a list of questions and asked to rate them, perhaps on a three-or four-part scale of "difficulty." But the panel approach has several problems.

How representative are the panel members? Are they experienced in the libraries about to be tested? If not, and it is unlikely that they will actually be from those libraries, how can their experiences be compared to the experiences of the librarians in the target libraries? Are they similar in intensity, duration, or frequency? Are the panel members likely to be comparable in education, motivation, or intelligence to the librarians who will be tested? Since they are likely to be chosen on the basis of their experience, expertise, or propinquity, it seems unlikely that they will resemble the librarians to be tested.

Once assembled, how consistent is the panel likely to be? We know that librarians in technical services are not perfectly consistent in their application of cataloging rules and that selection of subject headings for identical books six months after initial cataloging is significantly different. Panels of expert reference librarians are not routinely tested for consistency of judgment, nor are panels compared with other panels on the same questions to uncover regional, systematic, or random biases. Panels routinely identify some questions presented to them as too easy, others as too hard. There is no correlation with experience to determine if questions which panels identify as too easy or too hard are answered more easily or with more difficulty by their peers in the tested libraries. One of the most sophisticated reports of panel selection and judgment was given in Bunge's report of an obtrusive test given to librarians in five Illinois libraries in the mid-1960s (Bunge, 1967).

Following the selection and training of a panel, the questions were evaluated and selected, the proxies trained, and, finally, the questions applied.

QUESTION APPLICATION

The application of the questions varies along several dimensions related to time (busy or slack); and to proxy inquirer (age, gender, perceived status, motivation, purpose). What we do not know is how representative for the library being tested are the timing and proxy characteristics. For example, we know that most proxies are instructed to not be assertive or aggressive; if that causes them to be representative of a minority of patrons the service provided for them may not be representative of that provided for a majority of patrons.

The general question we are describing has to do with the tradeoffs which researchers make in order to make their research less costly and more efficient. Those tradeoffs are always assumed not to lessen the validity of the research, but they may. Consider the Hernon/McClure study. For reasons of economy, pairs of academic and public libraries were selected in 13 cities, rather than randomly chosen from the lists of the public and academic depository libraries. The latter course would have resulted in much higher research costs by increasing not only the travel expenses but also the time and living expenses of the researchers. But the tradeoff was not acknowledged; there is no mention of the assumption that question-answering and referral in libraries where there is another depository library in the same city is the same as that encountered in cities where there is no other depository library. The possibility of the two depository libraries cooperating on item selection and deselection, referral policy based on shared cooperative acquisition goals, or staff training is not mentioned, nor is the possibility that these areas of cooperation may well affect the reference question answering and referral practices of the two libraries.

Of course, researchers must compromise with their limited resources, and the ideal way to do a study is seldom, if ever, the practical way.

CONCLUSION

I have reviewed a few of the important aspects of research validity with regard to unobtrusive studies of reference question answering ability. Results of studies over the past 20 years have been remarkably stable. The libraries have been public and academic, the questions have been asked in person or by telephone; the subjects covered have spanned the range of classification; the sources used have varied from arcane government indexes to ubiquitous almanacs; and in a few instances, the librarians have even known that they were being tested. The question of the validity of the measures will always be important, but it seems unlikely that the general findings will be seriously challenged.

What does it all mean? Probably not that reference work as a whole is terribly flawed; the inability to answer the questions asked in unobtrusive tests may not relate very closely to the quality of other reference services such as bibliographic instruction. It certainly does not relate to the opinion patrons have of our helpfulness. Is it a cause for concern? Only if we think that the information we provide to our patrons is important, and that they care whether or not it is accurate. If the answers to those two questions are in doubt, then perhaps we had better rethink our basic mission.

REFERENCES

Benham, F., & Powell, R. (1987). *Success in answering reference questions: Two studies*. Metuchen: Scarecrow.

Bunge, C. (1967). *Professional education and reference efficiency*. Springfield: Illinois State Library.

Childers, T. (1987). The quality of reference: Still moot after 20 years. *Journal of Academic Librarianship, 13*, 73–74.

Crowley, T. (1985). Half-right reference: Is it true? *RQ, 25*, 59–68.

Dervin, B., & Fraser, B. (1985). *How libraries help*. Stockton, University of the Pacific.

Hansel, P. (1986). Unobtrusive evaluation for improvement: The CCPL&IC experience. *North Carolina Libraries, 44*(2), 68–75.

Hernon, P., & McClure, C. (1987). *Unobtrusive testing and library reference services*. Norwood, NJ: Ablex.

Rodger, E., & Goodwin, J. (1987). To see ourselves as others see us: A cooperative, do-it-yourself reference accuracy study. *The Reference Librarian*, No. 18, 135–147.

Ross, C. (1986). How to find out what people really want to know. *The Reference Librarian*, No. 16, 19–30.

Way, K. (1987). Quality reference service in law school depository libraries: A cause for action. *Government Publications Review, 14*, 207–219.

5

Do Library Systems Make a Difference?*

Thomas Childers

College of Information Studies
   Drexel University
   Philadelphia, PA

BACKGROUND

Systems. Systems of public libraries have existed in the United States for decades. While the systems are organized in different ways, their ends are the same: to achieve for the member libraries some benefits they could not realize alone.

It has been assumed that larger units of library administration lead to greater library effectiveness or efficiency—that more or better library services will result, or that the services will be provided more economically. Such assumptions, rarely *called* assumptions, have been expressed or implied for over half a century in writings advocating larger units of library service. So strong was professional conviction about the benefits of larger units of library service that standards for public libraries published in the 1960s were titled "Minimum Standards for Public Library *Systems*, 1966."

Assumptions. The assumptions have seen perhaps their most substantial manifestation in federal and state policies that have been written to improve the development and support of public library systems, consortia, and other larger units of service. Billions of federal, state, and county dollars have been spent implementing those policies. (Perhaps the most universally known policy statement came in the form of the federal Library Services and Construction Act, one title of which specifically fosters cooperative library efforts.) Like most other state library agencies, the State Library of Pennsylvania has devoted considerable energy over the past 15 years or so to the

---

   * By agreement with Jane Robbins, editor of *Library and Information Science Research,* and with author Thomas Childers, this chapter also appears in *Library and Information Science Research 4* (1988).

promotion of systems of public libraries in Pennsylvania, providing incentive money for the development and maintenance of systems.

Organization. The loosest organizational scheme for a system, and the one that allows the individual member library the greatest autonomy, is the *cooperative* system. The tightest organization, and the one that unifies individual libraries under a single administrative authority, is the *consolidated* system. Between these two extremes is the *federated* system, under which member libraries retain their autonomy, yet formally relinquish some specific responsibilities to a system administration.

Benefits. The assumed benefits of systems might relate to *services*, such as reference and information backup, access to materials, sign systems, programs, or reciprocal borrowing; to *operations*, such as materials selection, acquisition or processing, or circulation methods; or to *administration*, such as fund raising, political action, public relations, or staff training.

Reviews of the literature and contacts with selected state librarians indicate that, over the years, there have been very few attempts to determine the actual impact of system structures on libraries. Much of the attention paid to library systems has focused on their organizational details and on specific efficiency or effectiveness achieved or not achieved by individual systems. The studies have not included nonsystem libraries and thus cannot compare the relative achievements of system libraries and nonsystem libraries in order to assess the impact of systems. The age-old professional assumption that larger units of libraries, such as systems, are beneficial has not been adequately tested.

ADDRESSING THE ASSUMPTIONS

A study. In 1983–84, we[1] undertook a study of certain kinds of systems of public libraries in Pennsylvania to address some of the assumptions that underlie the professional predilection for public library systems. The summary research question was "Do public library systems in Pennsylvania make a difference in the effectiveness

[1] The principal investigator was Thomas Childers, Professor, College of Information Studies, Drexel University, Philadelphia, PA. Rodney P. Lane, affiliated with the University City Science Center, served as co-principal investigator. He is an expert in intergovernmental finance and a veteran library researcher. The study reported in part here is reported fully in Childers, Thomas & Lane, Rodney P. (1984). *An Evaluation of Pennsylvania's Public Library Systems*. Philadelphia: Center for Information Research, College of Information Studies, Drexel University.

or efficiency of public library services?" The purpose of the study was to provide sufficient information to the state librarian and the staff of the State Library of Pennsylvania to make informed decisions about the continued development of systems.

We deliberately excluded consolidated systems such as those of Pittsburgh, Philadelphia, and Erie and Mifflin Counties from the study, and included only the federated systems to which State Library attention and considerable State Library funds have been devoted for over two decades.

This chapter is a broad sketch of the problem and methodology for studying it and a selection of conclusions related to the impact of the system structure on Pennsylvania libraries. The actual data of the investigation are presented in the full research report.

METHODOLOGY

The accountability issue. The responsibility for being accountable to the public inheres in any public institution. As has been amply discussed in the literature, accountability in most public services, including public libraries, has been inadequate; and, thus, the empirical base for making policy regarding those services is inadequate. Generally, services are inclined to account for inputs to the organizations (organizational resources) rather than outputs, or performance. In part, this must be attributed to the reluctance or inability of the servers to invent valid measures of output and to the basic difficulty of doing so. It must also be attributed to the continuing willingness of the governors of public services to accept input accountability.

In many service sectors, as in public libraries, the nature of accountability has been changing dramatically, if slowly, over the past 20 years. Numerous writings document the library profession's progress through various stages of accountability. The field has matured from a stage of comfort with measures of library input, or resources, through the quest for measures closer to the library's output, or performance, to the achievement of some success and considerable promise in establishing such measures on a national scale. This degree of success has been realized through the work of many people in the library field over the past two decades. They have helped develop a construct of self-determinism and public accountability for public libraries and, more specifically, a process for establishing library goals and related output measures and, even more specifically, actual measures of output. One cannot contemplate this work without recognizing the pivotal role of Ernest R. DeProspo in conceptualizing the need for it, making significant advances in methodology, performing much of the data collection that has been done, and inspiring others to take up the output accountability cause.

Some constraints. In considering an evaluation of the impact of systems in Pennsylvania in 1984, several constraints were apparent that would in some ways limit our contributions to the public library's "new accountability." Primarily, the constraints limited the methodological advances we could make. Nevertheless, even an evaluation that used relatively old methods could add substance to the literature of public library accountability.

The constraints for the current investigation included the following:

1. A study would have to be ex post facto. Any "before" data must preexist or be gleaned from personal recollection.
2. Certain preexisting library statistics are notoriously unreliable. Statistics such as circulation and volumes owned have been shown in several studies to be irregularly reported. Although the statistics reported by Pennsylvania's public libraries to the State Library have not themselves been tested for reliability, they must be assumed to be similarly flawed. Calculations based on them must be suspect, to some degree.
3. A study sponsored by the State Library would have a relatively modest budget, which would not tolerate elaborate data collection such as intensive statewide interviewing, reviewing individual library records, or regathering library statistics.

Despite such constraints, the responsibility of the State Library to account for its library development policies and, particularly, policies governing systems development remained. Even in the face of questions about certain preexisting data and the limitations of ex post facto research, it was appropriate for the State Library to attempt an evaluation of the impact of its program of fostering and supporting public library federated systems.

Data gathering. Because of the constraints, we chose a multiple-operational approach—viewing the same phenomenon from several vantage points and through various methods. Thus, the evaluation rested on several kinds of data:

1. Site visits to selected system and nonsystem libraries.
2. An opinionnaire distributed to system administrators by an independent investigator six months prior to the beginning of this study.
3. Questionnaires to system administrators, system board presi-

dents, directors of system member libraries, and directors of nonsystem libraries.

4. Library statistics for system and nonsystem libraries in Pennsylvania reported to the State Library of Pennsylvania, 1970 through 1982.

5. Documentation of system funding levels and mechanisms.

SYSTEMS IN PENNSYLVANIA

Virtually all of the State's federated systems are organized on a county basis. Thus, some of the most important analysis could proceed on a county-by-county basis. At the time of the study, there was about an equal number of system and nonsystem counties in the State: 33 nonsystem counties (excluding Philadelphia) and 33 system counties. (Two additional subcounty systems exist, but they were removed from the evaluation, for the most part.) The systems, occurring in every region of the State, had a total of 218 local libraries as members. In 18 of the systems, *all* local libraries were system members. In the remaining 15 systems, a total of 33 local libraries were not system members. The system counties, most of which had been formed in the early and mid–1970s, served about 41% of the State's population.

FINDINGS

Site visits to selected system and nonsystem libraries; and the opinionnaire.

The study staff made site visits to 11 system and 3 nonsystem headquarters around the State. The systems were selected to represent a variety of organizational configurations and "levels of effectiveness." Coincidentally, an opinionnaire distributed independently (that is, by other than the study team) to all system administrators just prior to the current study sought opinion on major features of systems: their formation, organization, services, and strengths and weaknesses. Studying impact-related data from the interviews and responses to the opinionnaire enabled the study team to conclude that:

1. Systems serve a variety of functions, ranging from administrative and operational (such as technical processing and consultation

with member libraries) to direct service to library users (such as reference service and rotating collections).

2. The major strengths of the systems seemed to be their coordination and centralization of local library effort, and the increased financial backing that they have secured from county or State sources. The major weakness seems to have been the difficulty in building system-wide consensus, which is largely attributed to the autonomy of the local library in a federated system.

3. A major purpose of systems—their ability to bring additional financial support to the local libraries—appears to have been accomplished in different ways. To a major degree it is achieved by qualifying many local libraries for certain State aid, where they would not qualify on their own. To a modest degree, it is achieved by establishing a more effective unit—a coalition of local libraries—for pursuing increased financing at the county level. To a minor degree, it is achieved by increasing the visibility of the local library in order to acquire additional local funding.

Questionnaires to principal figures. A brief questionnaire was sent to a systematic sample of directors of system and nonsystem libraries and to the total population of system administrators and system board presidents. The purpose of the questionnaire was to describe perceptions of the present state and possible future of federated systems in Pennsylvania. One of the questions asked was relevant to the impact of systems on libraries and library services: "Over the past 1 to 5 years, how much assistance has *the public library system* given to *your library* in providing or improving the following *user services*? Circle the number . . . from 0 (none) to 4 (a great deal)." The services listed spanned the categories: materials available, programs, displays, materials circulated, interlibrary loans, reference/information service, services for special groups, and hours open.

Since people associated with systems have invested themselves in the system to one degree or another, one would expect them to be largely positive in their perceptions, and they were. Even so, the pattern of their responses offers some testimony to the impact of systems on libraries: For every user service listed (with the exception of hours open) over half of the respondents claimed that the system had provided or improved the service.

In the same series of questionnaires, directors of nonsystem libraries were asked the extent to which they thought a federated library system *might* provide or improve administration, operations or client services. The responses indicated that a federated system was generally seen as more likely than not to be of assistance, and to be of relatively more assistance in the area of client services than in administration.

LIBRARY STATISTICS

Two Questions and Two Categories

Library statistics that have been reported to and published by the State Library between 1970 and 1982 were analyzed. The statistics are not unlike those reported by many libraries across the nation to their state library agencies. While the reliability of the statistics is unknown and suspect, and while they do not represent all the kinds of statistics one would desire, they provide an additional point of view. The analysis focused on two questions:

1. What was the *amount* of change in selected variables in the system, as compared to nonsystem, counties in the 12 years?
2. What was the *rate* of change?

To focus the analysis, the statistics selected were divided into two categories: input, or resource, variables; and output, or performance variables.

INPUT VARIABLES
Number of libraries
Professional staff/1000 pop.
Operating expenditure/capita
Total income/capita
Local government income/capita
School district income/capita

Indirect federal aid/capita
Total local income/capita
State aid/capita
Federal aid/capita
Other aid/capita

OUTPUT VARIABLES
Number of books/capita
Volumes added/capita
Hours open/1000 population
Registration/capita
Circulation/capita
Interlibrary borrowings/1000 pop.
Interlibrary loans/1000 pop.
Circulation/volume

It may stretch the imagination to view "Number of books" or "Hours open" as variables describing a library's output, or performance. The study staff decided, however, that presenting a number of documents over a period of time constitutes a service to the client, and that the quantities of these things (volumes and hours open) are measures of that service. Even with such interpretations, one notes that the number of input variables, although only a selection from the reported statistics, exceeds the number of output variables, which includes all of the reported output statistics.

Analysis. Since the analysis consisted simply of comparing figures for system counties and nonsystem counties, and since we were dealing with the total population of the State's counties, figures were compared directly rather than through statistical inference.

Input. In terms of input, or resource, variables, there is no clear pattern of change over the 12 years when comparing system and nonsystem counties. That is, the statistics indicate no consistent impact of systemness on a library's resources. Variations from this general observation include the following:

1. System counties increased the number of libraries substantially more than nonsystem counties.
2. System counties made greater increases in the number of professional library staff. By 1982, they had fewer libraries without professional staff.
3. Nonsystem counties achieved greater increases in local municipal income.
4. Nonsystem counties also got somewhat greater amounts of income from school districts and increased that income at greater rates.
5. System counties received a somewhat higher and more consistent level of support from indirect federal sources (such as LSCA), as might be expected as the result of federal and State Library policies which rewarded systems financially.
6. System counties received larger amounts of federal aid.

Despite these variations, the rate of change of *total income* was similar for system and nonsystem counties.

Output. Comparing output variables of system and nonsystem counties as a group, the study staff found evidence that system counties improved somewhat more than nonsystem counties:

1. On three of the eight output variables, system counties gained in *amounts* more often than nonsystem counties: Volumes added per capita, Hours open per 1,000 population, and Interlibrary

loans per 1,000 population. On the remaining output variables, system and nonsystem counties were comparable in the amount of improvement.

2. In terms of the *rate* of change in output measures, system counties outperformed nonsystem counties in five of eight variables: Volumes added, Hours open, Registration, Circulation per capita, and Interlibrary loans. System and nonsystem counties were equivalent in two other measures: Interlibrary borrowings and Circulation per volume.

DOCUMENTATION OF SYSTEM FUNDING LEVELS AND MECHANISMS

An integral part of the overall study was to review the current pattern of funding for public libraries and public library systems. This review led to the following summary observations related to system impact:

1. There was a general parity of funding levels and income sources for system and nonsystem counties.
2. In securing funding at the county level, system counties made substantive advances that exceeded advances made by nonsystem counties.
3. The State Library's program of system development and support provided additional state-level funding to libraries that would otherwise not have qualified for it. These libraries were invariably small and not well supported at the local level. They have received benefits from system membership that nonsystem libraries have not.

Despite the general parity of system and nonsystem library funding, some differences appear in the proportions of revenue received from the various funding sources:

1. A larger portion of revenues was captured from *total local* sources (municipal, borough, school district) government by nonsystem counties than by system counties. Similarly, libraries in nonsystem counties received a slightly higher percentage of *local government* income than libraries in system counties, and a marginally higher proportion of *school district* income.
2. As one might expect, given federal and State Library policies, system libraries received a higher percentage of their income from *indirect federal* sources (such as LSCA).

3. As one would also expect, given the system-aid program of the State Library, system libraries received a higher proportion of income from *State aid*.
4. For most years of the analysis, system libraries received a higher proportion of their income from *federal aid* (such as revenue sharing).
5. Nonsystem libraries received a higher proportion of their income from "other" sources (such as endowment, fund raising, and gifts).

IMPACT OR NO IMPACT?

Negative impact. Overall, the investigation uncovered no negative impacts of systems. It is possible that they were disguised or that persons with negative assessments were shielded from the investigators despite our efforts to query the full range of attitudes and opinions. With the data at hand, we can only conclude that systems have had no or relatively little *negative* value for member libraries.

Resources. Regarding *resources*, systems seem to have made greater than average advancements in terms of library outlets and the number of professional staff since 1970. However, the message regarding fiscal matters is mixed. When system and nonsystem libraries are compared, some fiscal differences that seem to be related to the impact of systems stand out. First, a number of very small libraries have qualified for additional State aid for the first time. This is a statutory benefit that accrues through system membership. Second, libraries in some systems have made significant inroads on securing county support. This varies from system to system, but it is a pattern clearly associated with system membership. Other than these apparent impacts, there seem to have been few dramatic fiscal changes in system libraries compared with non-system libraries.

Client services. The relationship between systemness and provision of or improvement in client services is clearer. Since joining systems, the outputs of system libraries appear to have exceeded that of nonsystem libraries in two ways: They have recorded substantially greater increases in the levels of client services provided, and they have increased those levels at a substantially greater rate.

Positive impact. On balance, the evidence of this investigation points to a positive impact of the federated system mode in Pennsylvania—a positive impact that is not totally attributable to the statutory benefits of system membership, but might be attributed to something that happens when libraries are formally allied, administratively. Professional assumptions dating back at least 40 years were addressed by the data. The assumptions ascribed administrative, operational and—especially—service benefits to uniting libraries into larger administrative structures. Generally, the data support them.

The data also provide some support for the State Library's *general* policy thrust regarding the development and support of federated systems among public libraries over the past 20 years or so. The State Library has been justified, generally, in its fostering of systems.

POLICY DECISIONS AND SYSTEMS FEATURES

While the study explored the impact of State Library policy and operations on a scale unparalleled in the organization's history, only broad conclusions were permitted by the methodology. Policy makers still lack empirical data about the impact on library service patterns of *specific* policies for system development, or the implementation of those policies, and about the costs of improving library service in system and non-system settings. In the process of performing our study, it was clear that, over the years, a number of specific policies had cumulated into a macropolicy thrust that was somewhat unclear and of uncertain origin. Some of the specific policies were in potential conflict with one another. The investigators are convinced that better information about the impacts and costs of public library systems— even those in other states—would have permitted improved policy formation and oversight in the Pennsylvania instance. If the profession is to improve the information available to the people who make policy and decisions regarding public library systems, it is essential that we begin to search systematically for the relationships that exist between the features of systems and the outcomes of libraries.

6
Public Libraries: Flexibility and Political Action

Edwin Beckerman

Woodbridge Public Library
   Woodridge, NJ

THE "GOOD" LIBRARY

Some years ago, when chips were found on a poker table rather than in a computer, the late Ralph Shaw noted the tendency of library directors to generate a species of memoir he referred to collectively as "How I run my library good." You will, of course, still recognize this art form as alive and well, still kicking its way through the pages of library literature.

I suspect, however, that while Shaw may have intended his comment to be interpreted as a wry reflection on the tendency of individuals to generalize from their own "particulars," there is still a good deal to be inferred, beyond simple detail, from these biographies. After all, the question of "How I run my library good" always implicitly raises the larger question, "What is a good library?" Obviously the questions are inseparable. One cannot *run a library good* without defining the nature of a "good library."

Let me clearly limit the dialogue at this point to public libraries— those institutions which serve the entire population of a community. How does one define the concept of a "good library" in relation to service to an entire community?

Let me return to another Shaw for a moment—George Bernard, this time. In his preface to *Saint Joan* Shaw noted that every society draws its own line with respect to the beliefs and practices of individuals. With typical Shavian logic he outlines the conflict of a Joan, following her own inner voices and clashing directly with the need of society to protect its own value system. Without pursuing further the ethical or moral questions raised in *Saint Joan,* one might say similarly that society has its own point of acceptance with respect to its institutions. While this may not deal with issues of beliefs (although at times it does), a community constantly looks at its institutions and makes judgments, sometimes favorable, and sometimes not, and those institutions are indelibly marked by that judgment.

SOME OBSERVATIONS

I have spent a good part of my life looking at public libraries—my own as a staff member and director, and other libraries both as a state library consultant and later as an independent consultant. In all, I think it fair to state that I have probably worked directly, and often very closely, over extended periods of time with perhaps 150–200 libraries and library boards. While no libraries, boards, and communities are identical, I think it is fair to make some generalizations about communities and institutions on the basis of personal experience. I recognize, of course, that in the process of generalizing one describes conditions that do not pertain to every individual case. There is, after all, no inherent contradiction in recognizing that studies consistently document that smoking on the average will shorten life, while at the same time noting that some individuals who smoke intensively every day of their lives reach the ripe old age of a hundred and two. It should be recognized then that some of the following statements are intended to convey a general truth, but it is recognized that there will be exceptions.

PUBLIC LIBRARIES AND OTHER INSTITUTIONS

As I look at public libraries in most of the communities with which I am familiar, and as I compare them with the other public institutions which serve these communities, I am generally struck by the notion that public libraries have a large role in setting their own agendas and a great deal of flexibility in developing their own programs. I often sense a strong recognition of this by library interests (directors and trustees), and an equally strong desire to avoid any steps which may tend to restrict a library's freedom of action. This is particularly true of libraries which are isolated from the political process, or, more particularly, librarians and trustees who function outside of the political life of their communities. I am sure that many have heard expressed frequently in the past the view that the public library (read also public librarian and trustee) should remain aloof from politics, lest such contact tend to place political constraints on the freedom of action enjoyed by the public library. While it would be foolish to dismiss out of hand the fears and risks associated with closer interaction with the body politic, it is also true that many libraries endure their own more or less permanent self-exile on a desert island of their own creation, pure of action and empty of pocket. May I suggest in passing that integrity of action and involvement in a community political structure are not mutually exclusive.

To return to the main issue, it is my view that the function and field of action for most public institutions and activities in a community are much more clearly laid out and perceived than those of the public library. At least this is true of the perceptions of public officials and of the public in general.

THE PUBLIC UNDERSTANDS THE *OTHERS* BETTER

Let me contrast the operation of a public library in an "average" community with several other typical municipal services. I will avoid such services as sewers, since public perceptions of sewers tends to be nonexistent except in times of crisis. Road departments might provide one good basis for comparison. For the most part people in a community have a reasonably good view of what a road department does. It maintains the condition of the roads within a municipality. Views differ on how effective a job is being done by a given department (depending primarily on the condition of one's own local street) but there is little that is esoteric about exactly what one expects of that road department. Sanitation departments offer another point of comparison. Everyone has his own expectation of what he wants from a sanitation department. Pick up the garbage! Do it now! These simple injunctions reflecting basic primeval urges, of course, almost guarantee that few residents will ever be happy about the state of local service. The agenda of the local citizen, however, is very concrete, and the level of concern is high. Much of the agenda of both the road and sanitation departments is set with direct reference to public demand even though reality often falls short of demand.

Perhaps the best point of comparison between public libraries and other local public services is the local school system. As a rule local school systems are high in visibility, to say nothing of public expectations. Rare indeed is the local resident who has not a precise notion of exactly how a local school system should be run. The fact that a local consensus about the direction that local education should take is difficult to achieve does not detract from the strong visions of local education often held by the contending forces within a community. The compromises usually required to achieve resolution of such conflicts are driven to a substantial degree by the strong views held by the public as a whole. Thus local educational decisions are in a real sense either user-driven or, at the very least, substantially affected by user views.

In the three examples cited above, I believe that decisions are either clear-cut in terms of the issues involved or substantially affected by public reaction where controversy is generated. In general I believe these conditions pertain regarding local programs, but local public library operations appear to me to be something of an exception.

WHY ARE LIBRARIES AN EXCEPTION?

I remember a longtime colleague and veteran library lobbyist repeating a conversation with an influential legislator as follows: "I'd like to help you guys out but you gotta understand one thing. Libraries don't have no sex appeal." (If you're guessing this conversation took place east of the Mississippi you'd be right.) Public libraries are generally thought to be good things—polls consistently rank us between motherhood and apple pie—but not worth dying for. We generally have relatively low visibility, and, with the exception of some views about basics (providing books and reference service), there are few strongly held opinions on what public libraries should be doing. This is true of both the general public and of public managers and elected officials. Public library service seems often best defined by whatever it is that a local library does. Thus local libraries appear to be driven primarily by what they are currently doing, which fuels the level of public expectation, which, in turn, tends to support the current program of the library. Since current programs tend to mold public expectation, it is no wonder that public opinion samplings of local public library users not only disclose high satisfaction rates among local users, but in such overwhelming numbers as to court comparison with election returns in Bulgaria. (Do note, however, that few samplings query residents at large.) Of the many samplings of public opinion I have done at the local level, I can honestly say that the satisfaction rate expressed by residents regarding local library service bore almost no relation to how good the library was—good expressed here in the sense of size of collections, annual acquisitions, size of staff, hours of service, size of building. I will allow for some exaggeration in this statement, but far less than you might think possible.

If, in comparison to other local public services, public libraries are less defined than the others, if they tend to operate in a general climate of good will, but at times tend to function "beneath the notice" of some, if not most, of the public and of government, then they are faced both with some major problems and some major opportunities.

BAD NEWS AND GOOD NEWS

The bad news first. Local governmental services tend to proceed along well worn paths, and for quite logical reasons. Garbage does have to be collected, roads have to be repaired, police are needed for the maintenance of public order, and education is needed to prepare the young. In the judgments of the public and politicians alike, many municipal services are clearly essential. While libraries are well re-garded in a general sense, they are often considered "nice" rather than essential. They share this distinction with parks, recreation, and museums. Perhaps schools are the only class of institution affecting the human being above the neck which the body politic, to say noth-ing of the general public, finds essential. The battle for most public libraries is to secure a significant place on the agenda of a local community. Be quite certain, the agenda will only rarely automatically include libraries. Of course that does not mean that local public li-braries do not secure funding. It simply means that on the whole they are often not taken seriously, and often do not command the kinds of attention or support to achieve many of the goals librarians consider significant. How often have I heard a library board member or library director say, "They (local government) always give us what we ask for." Too often this self-satisfied note really reflects a terrible admission of abject failure: They never asked for anything worth refusing! And the reason they never asked for very much is that they implicitly recog-nized the library's rank in the scheme of things—low priority.

But, as I hinted earlier, there is some good news and some hope as well. As a kind of public institution, libraries may not have a high priority, but they are not without natural strengths. They are, as sug-gested earlier, generally regarded favorably by the public. If not as essential, they are regarded as important by at least some residents in a community. Moreover, as also already noted, they tend to set their own agendas. In a certain sense, it is not hard to *run your library good* since you (director, board member) tend to define what is good for the public. In effect, since the public tends to identify with the programs libraries provide, providing "good programs" allows for an almost certain success.

PUBLIC EXPECTATIONS

Before I address the major issue of program development, let me be very clear on this issue of program flexibility. There are, of course, expectations which the public has of their public libraries. There is a large core of service which the public expects, revolving around books, reference and research, and study space, and it is far from my purpose to deny this. Rather it is my judgment that, in general, the public lacks a fine sense of how libraries should proceed to provide these materials and services, lacks any common expectation as to how well services should be provided for them, and lacks a common view of what other services should be provided. All of this I perceive not in an absolute sense, but rather by way of comparison with other services provided to residents of local communities. With respect to these elements, the library itself has great flexibility in designing its own programs and affecting its own future.

IMPLICATIONS OF FLEXIBILITY FOR *RUNNING THE LIBRARY GOOD*

Assuming the accuracy of this perception, what is its implication? Presumably the existence of flexibility creates the possibility of alternative, informed choices. In a real sense freedom of action suggests the possibility of more effective action. How can one utilize this flexibility to "run one's library good"?

Let us begin with a cliché. All communities are different. They are alike in some, perhaps many, of their characteristics, but in a real sense they all have an individual dynamic that drives them. It is the librarian's (trustee's, friend's) job to understand where the community is, how it moves (or resists movement), and how the library relates to the community. Action must clearly be preceded by community analysis, and some degree of introspection regarding the library. Essential as well is some grasp of what is occurring in the library world at large, beyond the boundaries of the local community. We may have substantial local flexibility in program development, but this will be enormously enhanced by a broad perception of possibilities, a perception which will certainly be limited unless we have a broad understanding of what is happening in librarianship throughout the country and even the world.

Returning to the local picture, it is clear to me that public libraries, however much flexibility they possess, can only progress on a consistent basis if they recognize that they are a part of a community's political process and guide their actions accordingly. Public libraries are funded overwhelmingly through public sources, and this demands a political strategy, and, above all, the recognition that such a strategy is an essential tool if the library is to prosper.

Politics. What a nasty word—*politics!* Visions of smoke-filled back rooms, disreputable deals, and corruption come to mind. While this picture may be overdrawn, it is not without a basis in reality. Politics at the worst can, in fact, be what its critics charge, and the often-stated desire of library folk to avoid contamination is perhaps understandable. On the other hand, I would remind those so persuaded that probably little occurs in a smoke-filled back room that doesn't also occur in your average neighborhood corporate boardroom, in any organized institutions for that matter, including schools and libraries. Thus, those involved in libraries are always involved in politics of some kind. The only question is how far the range of this involvement extends and how well librarians and library advocates play the game of politics.

To those who will accept the fact that one of the major jobs of public library managers is to play the game of politics effectively, I will suggest that to do so the public library must have two kinds of goals and objectives. Service goals and objectives are essential for any kind of organized activity. Obviously one cannot reach a desired destination if none has been selected. (Equally obvious is the fact that many institutions have arrived at some goals, discovered only after having achieved them.) The second kinds of goals and objectives required by public libraries are, I believe, political. Call it political strategy. Service objectives and political objectives are intertwined and inseparable. Political aims are essentially means of achieving program goals, and political style is very much a part of program imperative.

In very narrow terms, institutions use politics (the art of gentle and often not-so-gentle persuasion) to convince the public at large and/or local, state, and national government that institutional programs are supportive of public welfare and absolutely essential to the public good. This is generally pursued in an atmosphere of some competition, since government does have practical financial limits and each governmental agency seeks to maximize its own position. As has already been noted, public libraries, when they enter this competition, have the advantages of a relatively broad field of action and a public which takes a generally benign view of the library. True, we are liked, but too often with something less than boundless passion, and we suffer the liability of low visibility. Given all of these cross-currents, how does the average library swim upstream against these often rapid forces?

The keys to developing both service and political objectives rest, I believe, in the nature of the community to be served. I think it is generally obvious to library practitioners that library services must be related to the public served by the library, and as communities differ, so must library services.

Political strategy and tactics. It is equally true that politics differ sharply from community to community and that, while political objectives of libraries may not differ markedly from community to community, political strategy and tactics certainly do.

The question of how a library functions in the political sphere relates both to the political style of the community and the posture of the library as it relates to the political structure. In some communities decision making is relatively broad-based and political processes, accordingly, are relatively open ones. In other communities the power and decision-making base is narrow. Power is relatively concentrated and easily identified. In some communities the public library appears to operate largely outside of the political structure. Where the public library is largely financed by public funds, this distance between the library and the political structure is usually more apparent than real. The real issue is apt to be not whether political strings exist (they do) but whether a library wields any significant political power of its own.

The important point is that developing a political strategy will depend on a number of variables, and it is important to take these into account. I cite below just a few of the more common issues that must be assessed.

Visibility. As already noted, most public libraries have low visibility from a political standpoint. This may be true for a variety of reasons. Many politicians do not use libraries and do not associate with library users. The closest they may come to library use is through their children, in which case they often think of a public library as primarily useful to children. This can be quite true also for nonelected public servants who have administrative control or influence. Before one can begin to deal with the question of library political strategy, one must assess the people who form the political structure.

Positive relationships. I am making the assumption here that greater political awareness of public libraries on the part of elected and appointed officials will generally lead to greater support, and I think this is so. Obviously it is necessary for the relationship between the library and the political community to be a positive one. Examples spring to mind of libraries which have had high political visibility of an entirely negative character. Negative relations between libraries and the political structure may sometimes be unavoidable in a good cause, but unnecessary hostilities should be avoided where possible.

Community-based strategies. To some extent, thus far, I have been discussing public libraries in a somewhat narrow context, and while I have done so to focus on particular elements of service, it is important to place public libraries in proper perspective. What the public thinks of its library is terribly important. While a community's view of its public library will rarely be negative, I believe that the *strength* of its attachment to its library will reflect their perception of its service effectiveness. Moreover, to a greater or lesser extent in most communities, the kind of library service provided affects the numbers and kinds of people who use it. Put it another way. Each community has a character and to the extent that we understand this community character we can plan to most closely develop our services to complement this character. For this reason service goals and political strategy are closely related. Understanding community composition and character enables one to develop effective political strategy which, if successful, will act to reinforce service goals.

I believe it is important to note here that while users tend to rate highly the library they use, the ability of libraries to reach large numbers of community residents will be directly affected by the character of their services. Thus, it is never useful to ask solely how well do *our patrons* like our service without also analyzing *total* community (non-users, too) reaction to the library (in business terms the degree and quality of the library's market penetration of its community).

Let me contrast the problem of the public library in two different kinds of political communities—narrow-based and open. I paint these pictures in their extremes—most communities are composites of both tendencies.

Narrow. The first community is narrowly based politically. Decisions are made by relatively few, and often the power group has held power for some time. Assume also that the library is not a member of the central decision-making group. What kind of useful approaches might be made? The answers are hardly esoteric! If there are organized meetings of other department heads, try to become part of such a management group. Often a library is already included in such management groups where they exist. Get to know other department heads. Find the occasion to talk to them individually. Get to know other municipal employees. It is often helpful. In smaller communities, remember everyone is someone's second cousin! One might assume this in larger communities as well. Get to know politicians also. When they've done something good—tell them. A successful election might well bring a letter of congratulations from a local library director, for example.

Above all, learn who has power. Particularly in a group with a narrow political base be conscious of:

1. Top budget officers and their assistants. Many of your key decisions will be provided by budget people.
2. Top administrators (managers, mayors).
3. Secretaries to top administrators. It is generally recognized that whoever controls access to those in power has a fair degree of power themselves.
4. Key people! Who are they? That is often the mystery. Keep all eyes and ears open, listen, see, read local newspapers carefully, and you will usually come up with a list of candidates who are capable of wielding a fair degree of power. Reaching them may be difficult at times, but if your library director and trustees get around their communities as they should, they ought to be able to establish some links.
5. One of the major problems that has existed in traditional political forums is that they have been almost exclusively male-oriented. For a male library director lifting a few at a local pub often served to cement some important relationships. Since many library directors have been female, in this and in other ways they have functioned under a severe handicap in not being able to move easily in an almost closed male society. Happily this is now changing, both because government is becoming far less male-oriented than it was only a few years ago, and because women are less willing to accept behavior on the part of males that was routinely accepted in the past.

Open. Assuming a much more open political process, with perhaps more frequent changes in both elected and appointed officials, I would first caution librarians to do all of the same things that they would do with a narrower based political structure. No government lacks a structure or a hierarchy. Find it and become part of it.

Beyond this, however, the question of developing an active and politically potent library constituency becomes one of overriding concern. I am not talking only, or necessarily, of developing a friends' group. I am talking about developing a core of community advocates who will exclusively, or among other concerns, focus on the library and its needs, and will communicate on a regular basis with local government.

While there are many ways of approaching the need cited above, I will concentrate entirely on one critical issue, which is crucial not only to political strategy and tactics, but to the central process of service itself.

Systematic observation. I have considered here the topic of relating service programs and political strategy to the nature of a community itself. I have taken this as a given, when all too often it is anything but that. While I would be the last to deny that developing a sense about the community one serves is partially a process of learning by osmosis, I would be concerned about the state of knowledge of any library director who has left it at that. Sixth sense is extremely useful, but it is no excuse for atrophy of the other five and no substitute for systematic observation.

Simply put, the more precise knowledge we have about our local community, its past history, its present demographic composition, its projected future growth, its attitudes, its use of the library, and its attitudes towards the library, the more clear we are about our goals, and the more effective are the tools at our disposal to help secure the kind of improved support that most of us so badly need. We have systematic approaches to community and service analysis available to us. The PLA Planning Process, the development of performance-based measures of service—much of which stretches back to the early work of DeProspo, Altman and Beasley (1973)—all have combined to provide the kind of disciplined approach to public library analysis that can prove of immense assistance to library practitioners.

THE ANSWER

The answer to my first implied question, "How do I know when I run my library good?" is probably that there is no answer. We have been struggling with this issue for as long as we have had public libraries, just as all institutions and individuals struggle with similar questions of values. I have suggested that as public libraries we have a better than average opportunity to run our libraries "good" because we have a fair degree of flexibility, and I have suggested as well that we have some recently developed analytical tools that can be of concrete assistance in analyzing library operations and community attitudes toward public libraries. Beyond that I have suggested that we look beyond our local communities at the programs and values we have developed as a profession. Ultimately I suspect that we will all wind up making our own individual value judgments about our own and other institutions. What one can hope is that these values develop in the broadest possible context, through reflection and exposure to knowledge and ideas, rather than in narrowness and isolation.

REFERENCES

DeProspo, Ernest R., Altman, Ellen, & Beasley, Kenneth E. (1973). *Performance measures for public libraries.* Chicago: Public Library Association.

7

Accountability of Library Services for Youth: A Planning, Measurement, and Evaluation Model

Shirley Grinnell Fitzgibbons

School of Library and Information Science
Indiana University
Bloomington, IN

INTRODUCTION

Though the literature of librarianship has been saturated with planning and evaluation models since the early 1970s, there has been no systematic attempt to apply these processes or models to library services for youth in public libraries. The major effort in this area by the American Library Association's (ALA) division, the Public Library Association, resulted in publication in the early 1980s of *A Planning Process for Public Libraries* (Palmour, Bellassai, & DeWath, 1980) and *Output Measures for Public Libraries* (Zweizig & Rodger, 1982). Though these manuals suggest that categories of users (such as children or young adults) can be differentiated when using specific measurement techniques as a second (and later) step, the importance and usefulness of doing so are not emphasized. Though new editions of each manual are now available (McClure, Owen, Zweizig, Lynch, & Van House, 1987; Van House, Lynch, McClure, Zweizig, & Rodger, 1987) youth librarians and the youth divisions have not been a part of the development process of these manuals.

Therefore, it will be the purpose of this paper to (a) show *why* it is important for library services for youth to be included in overall public library or community library planning and measurement processes, (b) to indicate why youth services have been basically left out of these processes to date, and (c) to adapt existing models into one useful for application to library services for youth. Though emphasis will be on the accountability of youth librarians (through a planning, measurement, and evaluation process) to both their institution, the public library, and to their clients, it will also be evident that a related issue is the accountability of the public library to two major user groups, children and young adults.

THE IMPORTANCE OF LIBRARY SERVICES FOR YOUTH

After a detailed analysis of user studies and national statistics on public libraries, Lawrence White concluded, "If student usage is added, current combined child and student uses [of public libraries] comes to about half of the total circulation" (White, 1983, p. 97). Though youth have always been a primary user group in public libraries, in today's information and technologically-oriented society, they need the public library even more. Major reports such as *A Nation at Risk* (National Commission on Excellence in Education, 1983), *Alliance for Excellence* (1984), and *Realities* (1984), have emphasized the importance of the information and learning needs of children and young adults as essential for the nation's future. For example, *Realities* designates Learning Begins Before Schooling as its number one reality. At the same time, *Alliance for Excellence* describes the retrenchment and erosion of resources in school library media centers. It is evident that, at least in some communities, the public library must assume a greater responsibility in providing youth with adequate space, open hours, materials, and staff to help meet their school-related as well as their personal information and learning needs and interests. It is also evident that public library services for youth is the way to help youth become lifelong learners and learn to view the public library as an institution which supports this process. Razzano (1985) reported an 85 percent correlation between those who visited libraries as children and continue to do so as adults in a survey of adult public library users in upstate New York.

The children's rights movement of the 1970s, which followed 300 years of a society with a philosophy of "protectionism" toward children, recognized that children and young adults have certain rights and needs. A youth's right to know and to have information in vital areas such as health and sexuality, even when the parent wants the information withheld, is an example of one of the major issues of the 1980s—the rights of youth versus the rights of parents.

Several court censorship cases have had to deal with school children's right to read and the right to information. Though there have been conflicting precedents, the judge in the *Right to Read Defense Committee of Chelsea* v. *School Committee* stated, "What is at stake here is the right to read and to be exposed to controversial thoughts and language—a valuable right subject to First Amendment protection" (Cole, 1985, p. 116). Though legislation and court decisions do not always uphold a youth's right to know, this ideology is a part of the library profession's ethics and one to which youth librarians usually subscribe.

An important concept has evolved from the children's rights movement, the concept of child advocacy, which has been explained by Gross and Gross (1977) as:

[W]orking with, or against, the systems that affect children . . . intervening in the process by which budget allocations or new legislation is made . . . tries to make our systems accountable for their actual effects on the lives of children. (p. 9)

Gross and Gross (p. 7) also speak of the "compelling mandate to every professional who works for and with children . . . . we must also consider ourselves child advocates." Both the Association for Library Service for Children (ALSC) and the Young Adult Services Division (YASD), two of the youth divisions of the American Library Association, have been increasingly interested in the role of youth advocacy for both their organizations and for youth librarians.

Youth advocacy as a concept can be translated in many ways in practice. Youth librarians need to become a part of the management team within the library, becoming involved in setting policies, planning and evaluation, and budgeting; they also need to work within the community with the schools and other youth organizations to insure that the holistic approach to youth needs is taken.

Unfortunately, children and young adults are usually viewed from the perspective of a particular discipline such as medicine, psychology, or education, or of a specific institution such as the schools, the courts, or social welfare agencies. This means that no one discipline or institution uses a holistic approach to the needs and interests of youth, with the result that some needs may be totally ignored. This becomes significant when one considers that there are approximately 68 million persons under 18 years of age in the United States and that in some states, preschoolers are the fastest-growing segment of the child population. Youth librarians need to be aware of changing demographics as well as new patterns of need such as the growing phenomenon of the needs of children in groups—in group care facilities such as preschools and latchkey programs.

Two essential differences between youth library services and those for adults are: the need in offering library services for youth to create an *expectation of services* (or creating demands) rather than responding to expressed needs and demands; and the need to base library services, including programming, on *developmental needs* ascertained by current theories from psychology, medicine, and education. The latter need will require the categorizing of youth by special age (developmental) groups, such as the two- and three-year-olds and the five-to-eight-year-olds when developing services. Though this is not always reflected in current practice, it is necessary in order to more effectively serve the total library and informational needs of youth.

THE IMPORTANCE OF PLANNING AND EVALUATION FOR YOUTH SERVICES

The accountability movement of the 1970s in government, education, and public services has pushed many libraries into planning and measurement primarily to justify budgets. Leaders in the school library media field, such as James Liesener (1976), David Loertscher and Janet Stroud (Loertscher & Stroud, 1976; Loertscher, 1979), and Evelyn Daniel (1976), have been concerned with concepts of program planning and budgeting, and they have developed models with applicability to the school library setting. Fred Pfister (1986) has presented, through one case study of a public school media program, a model of performance and program evaluation. Peggy Sullivan (1986) has suggested the application of measures from *Output Measures for Public Libraries* to school library media programs.

In the public library setting, similar application to library services for children and young adults has not been accomplished. The fact that children's library service has traditionally held a high status position in public libraries may have been a deterrent. Librarians who serve children may not have felt the need for planning and evaluation. Yet, trends of the 1970s, such as a decrease in the numbers of school-aged children in the population and improvement in school libraries in more communities, have resulted in lower public library circulation of juvenile materials as compared to adult materials and a de-emphasis in children's library services evident in less staffing and resources proportionately.

Young adult services have never been as strong as children's services in many public libraries even though this age group may compose about one-fifth of the population and has been a heavy user group of the public library. In many parts of the country, young adult library positions have disappeared, and few separate young adult coordinators exist, even in public libraries serving over 100,000 people. Neither children's nor young adult services have expanded in most communities; and it has been reported that in urban centers, these services have decreased.

Though it has always been important that public services be carefully planned on the basis of needs and use, libraries have been slow to adopt this practice. At a time when youth library services and resources are, at best, in a status quo condition, and when needs of youth are greater than these resources can fulfill, it is essential. The fact remains that in most public libraries, library services for youth are not systematically planned or evaluated. Yet the 1982 document of the Young Adult Services Division (YASD), "Competencies for Librarians Serving Youth" (Competencies, 1982), clearly states:

> (will be able to) formulate goals, objectives, and methods of evaluation for a young adult program based on determined needs (including) a. Design and conduct a community analysis and needs assessment, b. Apply research findings for the development and improvement of the young adult program, c. Design, conduct, and evaluate local action research for program development. (p. 51)

Neglect of Youth Library Services in Planning Processes

Definition. There have been several deterrents to inclusion of youth library services in planning and evaluation processes including: the problem of definition and delineation of youth user groups as unique user groups; the status, image, and role ambiguity problems of youth librarians; and the measurement problem itself—the debate over quality versus quantity.

Before one can consider planning or evaluation of services for any user group, the group must be operationally defined. This has been a unique problem in public library services to youth, especially in service to young adults who are not usually served in a separate area, with a special collection, or by a separate person. In most library research, measurement, or planning endeavors, at best only a single user category, juvenile, has been delineated. Current compilations of definitions, library glossaries, standards documents, and data collection manuals do not define children and young adults as separate user groups by either age or grade delineations (American, 1983; Lynch, 1981; Young, 1983). Even within two of the youth divisions of ALA, ALSC, and YASD, useful distinctions have not been made, though joint committees have worked on the problem. This ambiguity has added to the problem of planning and evaluation of youth library services and created a category of *invisible users.* (Without being counted as a separate user group, do you exist?)

Management savvy. Several library leaders have criticized children's librarians for their lack of a management orientation, for isolating themselves from the rest of the library, or for assuming inappropriate roles for today's society. For example, Pauline Wilson (1979, 1981) has criticized children's librarians for their lack of knowledge on how to set goals and objectives, how to measure and evaluate library services, and how to prepare, present, and justify a budget; she has recommended a clarification of their role, an examination of new roles as a result of societal changes, and improvement of the image of children's librarians to both librarians and society.

Status problems. Caroline Coughlin (1978) has objected to what she describes as the still pervasive nurturing role of children's librarians. Margaret Kimmel (1979) has explored the idea that librarians who strive for greater professionalism will treat lower-status clients less equally, and suggests that because children are often accorded less status as library users (by administrators, governing boards, other patrons), they may be treated less than equally by librarians. In her view, the current status insecurity of children's librarians may make them unable to fulfill personal and occupational commitments to the profession—and their commitment to children. Most youth librarians and others who work with youth recognize that because children and young adults lack political clout, they are often considered less important clients. Because youth librarians serve these less important clients they have both internal and external status and credibility problems.

Professionalism. Other problems involved with status and image involve the current national shortage of youth service librarians, the deemphasis in library education on training of children's and especially young adult librarians, and the current belief (and perhaps, mythology) that children's librarians have lower salaries, less career mobility, less prestige, and fewer fully professional positions. Though these aspects need to be explored further, it is not appropriate to do so in this chapter. They are, however, conditions that contribute to a major problem, the lack of full professionalization of youth librarians. The distinction between professional and nonprofessional responsibilities of librarians was first clearly spelled out in the ALA's policy statement on Library Education and Personnel Utilization:

> Professional responsibilities require special background and education by which the librarian is prepared to *identify needs, set goals, analyze*

problems, and formulate original and creative solutions for them; and to participate in planning, organizing, communicating, and administering programs of service for users of the library's materials and services. (*American Library Association,* 1970, unpaged)

Youth librarians have often not been involved in many of these professional responsibilities in public libraries, especially in small or rural settings. Statistics indicate that in many of these settings, children's librarians do not have the professional degree, the master's in library science. The lack of one or both of these two related factors, performance of professional responsibilities and the professional degree, probably contributes to the current status of youth librarians and may explain their noninvolvement in planning, measurement, and evaluation at the national, state, and local library levels.

Need for objectives. Though many librarians initially resisted the use of statistics to measure the effectiveness of services, youth librarians may have resisted measurement on the basis of their belief that the quality of their services was more important than the quantity usually measured. In addition, library services for youth have often been guided by global objectives and intuitive beliefs in the goodness of these services. The role(s) of the public library has changed over its history, with varying degrees of emphasis on educational, informational, cultural, and recreational roles. Youth librarians have reason to be uncertain about the appropriate roles and objectives of public library services without national or state guidelines and standards. While PLA has changed its approach to standards by the development of planning tools previously cited in this chapter, the youth services divisions, especially ALSC, has been without professional standards or guidelines for over 20 years. Meanwhile, the American Association of School Librarians (AASL) has prepared a new set of guidelines for their institutional setting after several years of dialogue on a national level concerning their appropriate roles and services (Information Power, 1988).

It is difficult to begin planning and evaluation processes without clearly defined statements of mission, role(s), and goals which can be translated into measurable objectives. It is also difficult to work toward improvement over the status quo without baseline statistics gathered at local levels and cumulated for comparison at state and national levels. Lynch (1985) has commented on the lack of statistics on library services to youth, both in school and public libraries, and has recommended that youth librarians through ALSC and YASD decide what data are useful (local, state, and national databases), define terms, and encourage librarians to collect and use the data. Then national and state agencies can be encouraged to collect and compare data.

There has been new interest in planning and evaluation on the part of youth librarians in the 1980s. For example, two articles recommending specific performance measurement for youth services have appeared: Gault (1984) for children's services; and Chelton (1984) for young adult services. There have been attempts to apply the *Output Measures for Public Libraries* to youth services. Two ALA committees have worked on the problem, PLA's Service to Children Committee and the ALSC/PLA Committee on Output Measures for Children's Services. Also, Zweizig and others in Wisconsin have completed an LSCA-funded project for field testing certain output measures for children's services in 20 libraries (Zweizig, Braune, & Waity, 1985).

Though attitudes of some youth librarians may have deterred their early involvement in planning and evaluation processes and other management roles, youth librarians are right not to simply accept the measurements and the evaluation processes which were developed for other settings, clienteles, and for adult-oriented services. Youth librarians do need to have a voice in the development of the important indicators of service effectiveness. Qualitative evaluation, which is gaining some credibility in other fields such as education, also needs to be more carefully considered for application to youth library services. In addition, the need for baseline and comparative statistics has been heralded, and some concrete steps have been taken. For example, the U. S. Department of Education sponsored a national Fast Response Survey System (FRSS) on library services to young adults in public libraries which has been completed and a similar survey on children's services is in process. For school libraries, the SchoolMatch database, with state reports released in 1987, clearly shows correlations between student achievement and library/media expenditures in public school systems.

PROPOSED MODEL FOR YOUTH SERVICES
IN PUBLIC LIBRARIES

The examples just cited focus on measurement of youth services, partly based on the use of output measures rather than on a total process of planning and evaluation, including measurement. Planning for library services for youth needs to be undertaken at the national, state, and local levels. Youth librarians need to be involved with all aspects of the public library but need to *lead in the planning of youth services*, including the identification of essential roles, goals, objectives, and services. There must be a process for developing some consensual thinking in each of these aspects.

Most influential in my own conceptualization of planning and evaluation processes has been the work by Ernest R. DeProspo, Ellen Altman, and Ken Beasley (1973) with performance measures for public libraries, the work of James Liesener (1976) with a planning/evaluation model for school library media centers, and the work in which DeProspo and Liesener collaborated (DeProspo & Liesener, 1975; DeProspo, 1976). The work of DeProspo and Liesener as a planning model for school libraries is especially adaptable to youth services within public libraries and can be used with or without the total library being involved in a planning process, though such involvement is preferable. Liesener's inventory of services, which was used as both an awareness device and as a tool for setting service priorities in school libraries, is the basis of my attempt to formulate and test several inventories for youth services.

A basic principle of the proposed model is that the intuition, experience, knowledge, and even informed opinion of youth librarians should be valued in the process. The process must begin with and finally answer the following questions:

1. What library services are needed by the total population of youth user groups?
2. What should be the mission and goals of youth services in the public library?
3. What are the most important roles for youth librarians?
4. What are the essential services and programs for youth?
5. Do effective services (cost-effectiveness) mean benefit and value to youth users and the community (cost benefits)?

The proposed model is presented in Figure 7.1 Proposed Planning Model for Youth Service in Public Libraries and includes three basic components: Steps in Planning Youth Services which have been adapted from the work of DeProspo and Liesener; the three Levels of Involvement—national, state, and local community; and the Types of Involvement—governmental, professional, and the various publics. The purpose of the model is to provide a systematic and rational framework for thinking about planning and evaluation of youth library services that will further professionalize the work of youth librarians in public libraries and improve youth library services. An expanded

Figure 7.1.   Proposed Planning Model for Youth Service in Public Libraries

Levels of Involvement	
Types of Involvement	Steps in Planning Youth Services
NATIONAL	PHILOSOPHY AND MISSION
—Governmental	
—Professional Organizations	INVENTORY OF ROLES
—General Public	
STATE	ASSESSMENT OF NEEDS AND USES
—Governmental	
—State Legislation	GOAL SETTING
—State Library Agency	
—State Education Agency	OBJECTIVE SETTING
—Professional Organizations	
—Library Associations	INVENTORY OF SERVICES AND PROGRAMS
—Education Organizations	
—Other Youth Organizations	PRIORITY SETTING
LOCAL COMMUNITY	
—Governmental	IMPLEMENTATION OF SERVICES/PROGRAMS
—General Public	
—Library Constituents	EVALUATION
—Library Board	
—Library Staff	LONG AND SHORT RANGE PLANNING
—Library Users including Youth	

explanation of the proposed planning model with draft inventories is in process and will be published elsewhere after it has been field-tested with appropriate groups.

The following inventories need to be developed: Inventory of Roles and Purposes, Inventory of Goals, Inventory of Objectives, and the Inventory of Services and Programs. An example of one draft inventory, the Inventory of Goals, is included in Appendix A. At this point, no separate delineation has been attempted for the two separate user groups, children and young adults; however, this is a necessary step in the process. Each of the inventories has been initially formulated by using standards and guideline documents, lists of competencies, and the literature of youth services.

Even though Figure 7.1 might appear to indicate otherwise, the process should not be considered linear, one-directional, or completely ordered. For example, the needs assessment and the use assessment must be done early in the process in order to describe the current situation; however, the two assessments will also be part of formulating the inventory of services and programs, and then they need to be repeated in the evaluation process. Certainly, the roles may need to be changed in view of an assessment of actual use and needs in a particular community with varying community services. The process is also an interactive process, both in the sequence of steps and in the involvement of many groups both within and outside the library.

Though *A Planning Process for Public Libraries* (Palmour, Bellassai, & DeWath, 1980) was oriented towards local community use, I suggest we need a specific youth services planning model for implementation at national and state levels as well as the local level. National and state level involvement is important because of the frequent lack of professionalization of youth librarians in many communities and because of the ambiguity and differing perceptions of the appropriate roles, goals and services for youth library services for the 1980s and beyond.

National Level Planning and Evaluation

In the proposed model, it is suggested that efforts should be made at the national level with government, with professional organizations, and with laypersons—the general public. Within the government, efforts should be made to mandate youth library services as a matter of public policy and concern, which should lead to gathering national statistics on youth library use patterns, to adequate funding of library services, and to national policy statements on library services to youth. This effort could be initiated through a project patterned after the efforts of the Department of Education which led to the report, *Alliance for Excellence*, through the National Commission on Libraries and Information Science, or through the establishment of a special advisory commission such as those leading to *A Nation at Risk* (National Commission, 1983) and *A Nation of Readers* (National Academy of Education, 1985). The National Center for Education Statistics (NCES) should begin to include categories of youth user groups in their periodic national surveys of public libraries. Baseline data on public library youth services is necessary for both evaluative and informational purposes. Monies need to be available for national surveys of the information needs of children and young adults, for the types of research recommended by the report, *A Library and Information Science Research Agenda for the 1980s* (1982). Adequacy of funding for youth library services needs to be assessed under such current legislation as the Library Services and Construction Act (LSCA) and the Education Consolidation and Improvement Act's Chapter II program.

Also at the national level, the American Library Association should

promote better library services for youth by making recommendations for a national plan, by developing standards or guidelines for
youth library services (all three youth divisions should work together
on such guidelines), and by working with other youth organizations in
areas of lobbying, legislation, funding, research, and planning. The
three youth divisions should initiate a dialogue among each other and
with the Public Library Association, the Association of State and Cooperative Library Associations, and the trustees' groups, using documents such as the proposed inventories, to seek some consensus on
the most appropriate roles and goals for both school and public library settings, individually and cooperatively, to best meet the needs
of youth.

State Planning and Evaluation

At the state level, a similar process should be implemented with governmental efforts, work by state library and education agencies, and
professional organizations. Youth library services should be targeted
in each state library's long range plan and in LSCA funding. State
library organizations should be involved with periodic surveys of the
state of youth library services, with developing standards and guidelines for service, and with establishing certification standards for the
educational background of youth librarians. These library organizations should work with the state library and education agencies to
promote more equitable and effective library services for youth.

Planning and Evaluation at the Community Level

The local community level is the most important level of planning in
terms of impact; however, because there are so many youth librarians
who are not in full professional roles, they may not be assuming the
leadership role they should in initiating planning activities. Because *A
Planning Process for Public Libraries* is directed toward local planning, the manual can be used as a framework for planning youth
services, especially some of the processes such as setting up committees, designing surveys, and finding community information. It is
recommended that youth services committees be included. Though
space will not allow a discussion of each step in the proposed planning process, the following suggestions are offered:

1. There should be substantial feedback from national and state
    planning processes to support local planning. Those involved in

local planning should not wait for such efforts. Each effort can and should be simultaneous and continuing.

2. The uniqueness of each community should be considered in the modification of each of the draft inventories.

3. There should be full involvement of all the constituencies outlined in the model with leadership asserted by youth librarians. When there are no professional youth librarians at a local level, a consultant should be considered or the effort should be made at the network level.

4. A concerted effort should be made to collect baseline data on youth services and to systematically survey these services over time. Local statistics should be fed into the state database and the Office of Education should include youth library services in each national public library survey as well as periodic special surveys such as the FRSS of young adult library services.

5. Attempts should be made to measure the benefit and value of youth library services (cost benefit) as well as the effectiveness (how good youth services are). These efforts should be made with the expertise and objectivity of researchers. This will require joint planning and work of youth librarian practitioners with youth library researchers.

The four inventories listed earlier (in process) such as the sample Inventory of Goals (see Appendix A for goals and Appendix B for references) should be utilized by the various constituencies described in the model in the following way: First, a discussion of each of the items is needed, with the right to discard items not considered appropriate in a particular community, and to add items considered more appropriate. Second, ranking of the final items in each inventory should occur, using either the Liesener point system or placing each item in one of the following categories: essential, important, or desirable. Third, consensus should be sought for each inventory. And fourth, performance indicators for each objective should be developed.

Evaluation and Measurement

Evaluation, including measurement, should be continuous and interactive during the total planning process. Both quantitative and qualitative evaluation are essential to adequately assess the effectiveness of services and programming for children and young adults. When appropriate, performance evaluation with the use of output measures should be used so that youth services can be compared with adult services within one library and compared between libraries. Once the roles, goals, and measurable objectives have been ascertained, the appropriate evaluation techniques can be determined. Previous work in this area should be considered as a building block. For example, the Wisconsin project pretested the following output measures with children's services:

1. Library Registration of Juveniles as a Percentage of Juvenile Population
2. Juvenile Library Visits per Juvenile Capita
3. Juvenile Circulation per Juvenile Capita
4. In-Library Use of Juvenile Materials per Juvenile Capita
5. Turnover Rate of Juvenile Materials
6. Reference Fill Rate for Juveniles
7. Annual Juvenile Program Attendance per Juvenile Population (Zweizig, Braune, & Waity, 1985).

Mary K. Chelton has identified an additional four measures for young adult services: autonomous success rate, collection appropriateness, youth participation rate, and proportion of cross-age programs (Chelton, 1984). Other useful measures I would recommend include information transactions per juvenile user; juvenile library visits per service hours; juvenile program attendance per age user group/per juvenile population; and title, author, and subject fill rates. Though the emphasis currently is on separation of a juvenile category from the adult category, it would be more useful to divide juvenile into categories by age (or grade) levels. A minimum breakdown should include: children, 1 to 12 years of age; and young adults, 13 to 18 years of age. For some statistics and measures, further breakdowns should be attempted such as preschool and ages 5–8.

In addition to the quantitative measures for programming, other useful evaluation could include written or verbal responses from the youth group, from the parents or other attending adults, and from the youth librarians. These anecdotal comments should be recorded along with the program description, objectives, and target audience. For each program or service, critical success factors should be determined. The combination of quantitative and qualitative evaluation can be a powerful tool in determining effectiveness.

FUTURE DIRECTIONS

Because this chapter was first written in 1985 with several revisions undertaken through 1988, it is important to list several ongoing related developments.

First, the National Center for Education Statistics Survey Report on "Services and Responses for Young Adults in Public Libraries" was issued in July 1988. This survey, referred to earlier in this chapter as the Fast Response Survey System (FRSS), is the first attempt to describe the status of young adult library services nationwide, an important statistics gathering effort stimulated by the efforts of the Young Adult Services Division (YASD). In addition, the Association for Library Service to Children (ALSC) reports, in the December 1988 *ALSC Newsletter*, that a similar questionnaire is in preparation for children's library service.

Second, a draft report of the ALSC Education Committee, "Competencies for Librarians Serving Children in Public Libraries" (1988), includes under the category of Administrative and Management Skills, several planning and evaluation competencies. The development of these competencies statements is important and complements previous work on similar competencies by YASD.

Third, the ALSC/PLA Joint Committee on Output Measures for Children's Services presented to the two divisions' Executive Committees in October 1988 a proposal for a project to adapt and enhance Output Measures for measuring and evaluating library services to children. This project will need funding and, if it proceeds, will probably need at least two years' work to produce the product the group envisions. It is not only appropriate that such a joint committee undertake this project, but the project is vitally needed to bring youth library services in line with other public library measurement and evaluation efforts.

And fourth, the University of Wisconsin-Madison's School of Library and Information Studies has received funding from the U.S. Department of Education for an institute in May 1989 on "Evaluation Strategies and Techniques for Public Library Children's Services."

These efforts on the part of professional organizations, government, and library education, are indeed positive signs for the 1990s and beyond for youth library services.

CONCLUDING REMARKS

In my view, library services for youth must be given a higher priority at the national, state, and local levels. The importance of these services must be proven to legislators, administrators, governing boards, the library profession, and the general public. Evidence must be presented to each of these constituencies based on: research in areas such as developmental needs, and the impact (value) of libraries, reading, media, and technology on youth; statistics collected at local levels on current services and needs; and the recommendations of commissions and professional groups who have been involved in the planning model described. This kind of evidence can only be accumulated as a result of a systematic planning process, and only when youth librarians recognize this need and assert a full professional role in its implementation will they be truly accountable to their clients, and their institution. The public library should recognize its vital role in providing library service to youth, and become accountable as a public service agency. Lawrence White has provided evidence that:

> Service to children and students comes closest to satisfying the library's goals of encouraging literacy and furthering education; . . . the case for public provision of free library services is at its strongest when applied to children's and students' service. (White, 1983, p. 99)

REFERENCES

Alliance for excellence: Librarians respond to a nation at risk. (1984). Washington, DC: U. S. Department of Education.

American national standard for library and information sciences and related publishing practices—Library statistics, ANSI Z39.7. (1983). New York: American National Standards Institute.

American Library Association. (1970). *Library education and personnel utilization.* Chicago: American Library Association.

Chelton, Mary K. (1984). Developmentally based performance measures for young adult services. *Top of the News, 41,* 39–51.

Cole, Terry W. (1985). Legal issues in library censorship cases. *School Library Media Quarterly, 13,* 115–122.

Competencies for librarians serving children in public libraries. (1988). *ALSC Newsletter, 9,* 3–4.

Competencies for librarians serving youth. (1982). *SLJ, School Library Journal, 29,* 51.

Coughlin, Caroline. (1978). Children's librarians: Managing in the midst of myths. *SLJ, School Library Journal, 24,* 15–18.

Daniel, Evelyn. (1976). Performance measures for school librarians: Complexities and potentials. In M. Voigt & M. Harris (Eds.), *Advances in librarianship* (pp. 2–53). New York: Academic Press.

DeProspo, Ernest R., Altman, Ellen, & Beasley, Kenneth E. (1973). *Performance measures for public libraries.* Chicago: American Library Association.

DeProspo, Ernest, & Liesener, James. (1975). Media program evaluation: A working framework. *School Media Quarterly, 3,* 289–301.

DeProspo, Ernest R. (1976). A program planning and evaluation self-instructional manual. In J. Liesener (Ed.), *Media program evaluation in an accountability climate: Proceedings of the AASL Program, San Francisco, June 29, 1987.* Chicago: American Library Association.

Gault, Robin. (1984). Performance measures for evaluating public library children's services. *Public Libraries, 23*, 134–137.

Gross, Beatrice, & Gross, Ronald. (Eds.). (1977). *The children's rights movement*. New York: Anchor Books.

Information power: Guidelines for school library media programs. (1988). Chicago: American Library Association.

Kimmel, Margaret. (1979). Who speaks for the children? *SLJ, School Library Journal, 26*, 35–38.

A library and information science research agenda for the 1980s: Final report. (1982). Santa Monica, CA: Cuadra Associates, Inc.

Liesener, James. (1976). *A systematic process for planning media programs*. Chicago: American Library Association.

Loertscher, David. (1979). *MEDIA IOWA: Media centre program evaluation document for Iowa area education agencies*. Des Moines, IA: Iowa Department of Public Instruction.

Loertscher, David, & Stroud, Janet. (1976). *PSES, Purdue self-evaluation system for school media centers*. Idaho Fall, ID: Hi Willow Research and Publishing.

Lynch, Mary Jo. (1985). Statistics on library services to youth. *Top of the News, 41*, 181–183.

Lynch, Mary Jo. (Ed.). (1981). *Library data collection handbook*. Chicago: American Library Association.

McClure, Charles R., Owen, Amy, Zweizig, Douglas, Lynch, Mary Jo, & Van House, Nancy. (1987). *Planning and role setting for public libraries*. Chicago: American Library Association.

National Academy of Education. Commission on Reading. (1985). *Becoming a nation of readers: The report of the commission on reading*. Pittsburgh, PA: National Academy of Education.

National Commission on Excellence in Education. (1983). *A nation at risk: The imperative for educational reform*. Washington, DC: U.S. Department of Education.

Palmour, Vernon E., Bellassai, Marcia, & DeWath, Nancy. (1980). *A planning process for public libraries*. Chicago: American Library Association.

Pfister, Fred. (1986). An integrated performance evaluation and program evaluation system. *School Library Media Quarterly, 15*, 61–66.

Razzano, Barbara Will. (1985). Creating the library habit. *Library Journal, 110*, 111–114.

Realities: Educational reform in a learning society. (1984). Chicago: American Library Association.

Sullivan, Peggy. (1986). Performance standards for SLM centers: Taking the initiative. *SLJ, School Library Journal, 32*, 48–49.

Van House, Nancy A., Lynch, Mary Jo, McClure, Charles R., Zweizig, Douglas, & Rodger, Eleanor R. (1987). *Output measures for public libraries*. Chicago: American Library Association.

White, Lawrence. (1983). *The public library in the 1980s*. Lexington, MA: Lexington Books.

Wilson, Pauline. (1979). Children's services in a time of change. *SLJ, School Library Journal, 25*, 23–26.

Wilson, Pauline. (1981). Children's service and power: Knowledge to shape the future. *Top of the News, 37,* 115–125.

Young, Heartsill. (Ed.). (1983). *The ALA glossary of library and information science.* Chicago: American Library Association.

Zweizig, Douglas, & Rodger, Eleanor J. (1982). *Output measures for public libraries.* Chicago: American Library Association.

Zweizig, Douglas, Braune, Joan, & Waity, Gloria. (1985). *Output measures for children's services in Wisconsin public libraries: A pilot project—1984–85.* Madison, WI.

APPENDIX A
INVENTORY OF GOALS
FOR LIBRARY SERVICES FOR CHILDREN AND YOUNG ADULTS*

1. The public library should establish library services to meet needs of children and young adults considering the developmental needs of each age group and other community services available.

2. The public library should maximize the accessibility of information resources to the potential youth library user.

3. The public library should serve as an auxiliary agency to the school-related needs of youth.

4. The public library should provide information and materials to fulfill personal, recreational, and social needs of youth.

5. The public library should encourage, stimulate, and provide for reading needs and interests of age groups including preschoolers through high school students.

6. The public library should encourage habits and patterns of lifelong library use.

7. The public library should provide opportunities for all youth to:

   • expand their knowledge
   • further search for understanding of self and environment
   • satisfy need for aesthetic experiences
   • develop pride in heritage and appreciation of other cultures
   • improve ability to make critical judgments
   • develop their verbal, visual, and aural communication skills.

8. The public library should reach beyond its facility, to extend library services to all youth within the community.

---

*This is a draft inventory of goals and not considered either inclusive or exclusive.

9. The public library should serve as an advocacy agency for needs and rights of children and young adults.
10. The public library should both cooperate with other community agencies concerned with youth services and act as a referral agency.

APPENDIX B
REFERENCES USED IN DEVELOPING DRAFT INVENTORIES

American Library Association. (1978). *Directions for library services to young adults*. Chicago: American Library Association.

American Library Association. (1975). *Look, listen, explain: Developing community library services for young adults*. Chicago: American Library Association.

Benne, Mae. (1978). Educational and recreational services of the public library for children. *Library Quarterly, 48*, 499–510.

The changing role in children's work in public libraries: Issues and answers. (1977). Detroit: Detroit Public Library.

Chelton, Mary K. (1978). Educational and recreational services to the public library for young adults. *Library Quarterly, 48*, 488–498.

Children's Services in Libraries and School Media Centers Division, Ohio Library Association. (1984). *A guideline to planning public library service to children in Ohio*. Columbus: Ohio Library Association.

Community Library Services—Working Papers on Goals and Guidelines. Task Force on Children's Services Working Paper. Task Force on YA Services Working Paper. (1973). Chicago: Public Library Association.

Goals, Guidelines, and Standards Committee, Public Library Association, American Library Association. (1979). *The public library mission statement and its imperatives for service*. Chicago: American Library Association.

Kingsbury, M. E. (1978). Goals for children's services in public libraries. SLJ, *School Library Journal, 24*, 19–21.

Long, Harriet G. (1953). *Rich the treasure*. Chicago: American Library Association.

Public Library Association. Committee on Standards. (1964). *Standards for children's services in public libraries*. Chicago: American Library Association.

Public Library Association. Committee on Standards for Work with Young Adults in Public Libraries. (1960). *YA services in the public library*. Chicago: American Library Association.

Young adults deserve the best: Competencies for librarians serving youth. (1982). Chicago: YASD Education Committee, Young Adult Services Division.

Young, Diana. (1986). Services to children in groups. *Public Libraries, 25*, 100–104.

Youth Services Section, New York Library Association. (1984). *Standards for youth services in public libraries of New York State*. New York: New York Library Association.

8

The Accountability of Public Organizations for Educational Projects Supported by Grant-Making Agencies

Thomas C. Phelps

Senior Program Officer
   National Endowment for the Humanities
   Washington, DC

IMPACT OF PROGRAMS ON CLIENTS

Most agencies that provide support for discrete educational programs for either targeted groups or for general public audiences require both an analysis and evaluation of such programs. Because of this requirement, public organizations must develop methods for analyzing and evaluating their programs and present these methods to the funding agencies at the time they make a request for support. More often than not, public organizations present evaluation plans that offer to count only the number of clients served, the number in attendance, the number of questions asked by clients and the like. Seldom is it the case that public organizations present an evaluation plan that makes an attempt to measure the impact of their program on the audience described. Moreover, public organizations seldom present a methodology for process evaluation to prospective funding agencies because such methodologies usually suggest that project objectives could be altered or changed. Changing the charted course, public organizations presume, would be viewed by supporting agencies as ambiguous, doubtful, or uncertain; ergo, support from a grant-making agency would be denied or withdrawn if plans appeared to be ambiguous.

Because questions that would measure the impact upon clients of services provided by public organizations are often not formulated, and because process evaluation is often ignored in the plans for evaluating discrete programs, public organizations are, perhaps, not as accountable to funding agencies as might be possible. Similarly, funding agencies, since they cannot present hard evidence regarding success or failure, are not as accountable as they could be to trustees or other governing bodies if better reports regarding the projects they supported were submitted. If methodologies were devised that would measure projects during their progression toward stated objectives and again at the end of the project in terms of products and impact, both the public organizations and the grant-making agencies could demonstrate trends, indicate reasons for success or failure, and in other ways document a clear accountability for use of funds.

SOME ATTEMPTS TO SHOW ACCOUNTABILITY

Early in the 1960s, departments and colleges of political and social sciences at American universities began to develop precise measures for the accountability of public agencies, measures intended for the use of public and private sector. Translating these measures for accountability from academic contexts to public agency use, however, was a difficult task—a task requiring both expert academic knowledge and an understanding of public organizations on the part of those who would attempt such a translation. Dr. Ernest DeProspo, who held a Ph.D. in political science from the Pennsylvania State University and was on the faculty of the School of Communications, Information and Library Studies at Rutgers, The State University of New Jersey, attempted to put the theories of public organization accountability into practice at public institutions, especially libraries. Measures of accountability were incorporated into the planning process for the services provided by 10 libraries as early as the late 1960s. Performance measures developed by DeProspo and others attempted to make generalizations about clientele, and· through these generalizations, measure the services that institutions provided to them.

In October of 1973, another methodology was introduced for the measurement of services through a process evaluation. This methodology, *Program Planning and Evaluation*, developed by DeProspo (1973) and issued by the College Entrance Examination Board, could be used not only for all operations of large public organizations, but also for smaller, discrete projects such as those supported by funding agencies and those not necessarily part of an institution's long standing, ongoing services.

At libraries, the educational programs, exhibitions of materials, and reading and discussion programs are examples of programs that are, perhaps, ancillary to ongoing information and reference services. These kinds of programs are, nonetheless, carried out as part of the institution's mission and are rightful activities for measurement.

Program Planning and Evaluation (PP&E) is an effective tool because it provides a model to measure both the process of a discrete project and the impact of such programs for an identified clientele. PP&E provides a logical sequence of events for planning and evaluating programs. It implies a process, and the process implied is evolutionary because it develops (or unfolds) gradually, and each step after the first relies on the development, measurement, and evaluation of the preceding steps. PP&E, as a process, should begin at the earliest stage—the planning stage—in the design of any program.

More about PP&E as a Tool

As a model, PP&E could be used as an effective tool for planning and evaluating discrete programs of library service for the general public. Prospective applicants to the Humanities Projects for Libraries and Archives program at the National Endowment for the Humanities are encouraged to employ a program planning and evaluation method in the design, planning and implementation of projects. Applicants are encouraged to consider a methodology for assessing and, perhaps, evaluating a project's value and impact on clientele. Methodologies for assessing "impact," "value," "importance," "melioration," "betterment," "learning," and the like cannot always be empirical. (For example, short of "pre-test–post-test" methods, how can one observe what is learned by a person as he or she passes through an exhibition?) The method outlined in DeProspo's PP&E monitors actions taken to provide a program. These actions, taken to provide a service to the general public, are observed in order to assess whether or not the service is being provided through the actions. In some cases, the effectiveness of the service can be measured, but not always. Again, for example, if the service is to provide an "understanding of historical ideas, figures or events" or to provide an "appreciation of cultural works," it is enough to know that actions meet the objective of providing the "service," but "appreciation" or "understanding" do not need to be measured for "effectiveness."

Applicants are advised to use a program planning and evaluation methodology because it allows for planning, assessing needs, projecting goals, writing objectives, listing actions needed, prescribing alternatives to those actions, and providing a time for the selection of actions or their alternatives along the way.

Early on, a methodology like PP&E forces program planners to ask "Whom is the program for and what will the program give to them?" It does not immediately address the questions usually asked at the end of a project: "How many came? How did they like it?" Nor does PP&E allow program planners to begin by thinking they know best what is needed. Instead, planners must ask: "What do we have? Does someone need it? How should we convey it to them?" These questions are ideal for programs that are for the general population.

PP&E and Funding

Programs supported by Humanities Projects in Libraries at NEH should conform to a public need already defined by the Congress of the United States: "Democracy demands wisdom and vision in its citizens" (National Foundation on the Arts and the Humanities, 1970, p. 1). Programs supported by Humanities Projects in Libraries must also be designed to fulfill the Endowment's legislative mandate "to foster public understanding and appreciation of the humanities" (National Foundation, 1970, p. 1) through public programming in libraries using the collections housed in libraries in order to convey "wisdom and vision" to the citizenry through the study, reading and interpretation of those collections. Essentially, the *need* is already defined by the U. S. Congress, and moneys are appropriated to meet this need. Using PP&E, several libraries have planned programs and received support to provide an "understanding of historical ideas" or an "appreciation of cultural works."

In one library, librarians and their trustees determined that "Printing and Censorship" was a topic that, if illuminated, would confer upon or offer to citizens some "wisdom," some "vision" for a better understanding of their world and culture, thereby fostering good judgment for an enhanced democracy. Using methods of program planning and evaluation, a project on "Printing and Censorship" was launched at one of this nation's largest public libraries. Owing largely to the process and summative evaluation of that project, programs were subsequently taken nationwide, to many cities and towns.

In order to carry out such a project, goals and objectives, action steps and alternatives to those actions were established from the beginning. In short, a systematic process for determining direction and evaluating results through the identification, clarification, and communication of goals and objectives for the project was used in order to "measure" the project, set its parameters, defined its context, and indicated its products, read as follows:

Over the next year and one-half, the New York Public Library will develop and implement a series of public education programs and exhibitions which use the Library's collections as a basis for critical examination of two broad issues: 'printing' and 'censorship.' Highlighting selected portions of the Library's holdings, the exhibitions will reach back to ancient thought, through the Renaissance, Enlightenment, and the transformations of the 19th and 20th centuries. The exhibitions will each form the basis for a catalog, a series of public lectures and discussions, and a collection of essays. (Gregorian and Schull, 1983, unpaged proposal)

After having stated the goal for the "Printing and Censorship" project in broad terms of intent, constrained only by time, the project's objectives were established. The objectives were specific statements, which described what needed to be accomplished, described work that needed to be completed, and indicated who would do the work. Examination of the objectives written for the project follow:

1. The library will prepare and install a large-scale exhibition, entitled 'Printing and Censorship,' in the library's newly renovated exhibition hall, for the general public to see, to understand, and to appreciate. The library's exhibition curator, along with chosen scholars, will select material from the library's collections, prepare the interpretive texts for both the exhibition and the publications, and design, develop, and supervise the fabrication of the exhibition to conform to six particular historical eras.

2. The curator and the chosen scholars will also be responsible for the intellectual content of the exhibition. Under the supervision of the curator, with consultation from the scholars, the exhibition will begin with a section designed to serve as both introduction and conclusion. Using Milton's *AREOPAGITICA* and Orwell's *1984* as the key references, this section will set forth the themes of the exhibition and define its historical and geographical boundaries. Four basic themes—Religious, Scientific, Political, Moral—which distinguish types of censorship over time will be shown to have had parallel courses with shifting emphasis, through the six major sections of the exhibition. These themes will contribute the threads for understanding what could and could not be said or written at different times and in different places. Through the choice of lead texts, graphics, images and arrangements, the exhibition will explain which of these themes predominated in particular eras.

3. Several scholars, the curator, and the library's coordinator of educational programs will be responsible for developing and presenting a series of lectures, discussions and debates on issues of censorship emerging from the prepared interpretation of the exhibition. The lectures on selected themes relating to censorship will be prepared and

given by scholars, who will also lead discussions. The coordinator of educational programs will schedule the programs at the library and its branches at times convenient for the general public.

4. The curator and the scholar-advisers will be responsible for the development and publication of an exhibition catalog, and for the development and publication of a series of essays from the prepared papers and lectures given during the public programs. Each of these publications will be made available to the general public for future reference and study, either free of charge or at a reasonable rate (Gregorian & Schull, 1983, unpaged proposal).

The actions needed to carry out the project's objectives were carefully laid out and put into a time frame. As each of the actions was taken, they were evaluated before the next action steps were selected. In one case, a whole subset of programs on "printing" was discarded because it did not relate specifically enough to the overall program topic of "Censorship." By making decisions based on previous actions, *process* evaluation took place at every step of the project. The library was accountable to NEH, the funding agency, every step of the way, also ensuring fiscal accountability. The money was well spent and the project met both the needs of the host institution and the parent, the funding agency. Another measure was ultimately used: How many saw the exhibit. How many came to the programs? Indeed, thousands of people came to the exhibition, and hundreds attended the programs. This count, however, does not measure what was learned. It only shows that an opportunity to learn was provided. Observing those who went through the exhibit and watching those who sat in the educational programs led observers to conclude that many people learned much about censorship from a positive, historical perspective. The public was given an opportunity to study a topic, and through that study, to better understand and more fully appreciate an aspect of the humanities, thereby meeting the public mandate for NEH. The public was also given the opportunity to share in the wealth of the rich holdings stored in the collections of their library.

PP&E: A Preferred Model

Using models for process evaluation, "evaluating as we go," is generally accepted by grant-making agencies, be they public or private, as a method of accountability; indeed, more and more often, process evaluation is preferred. Using models such as PP&E, grant seekers are writing better proposals and submitting them in the competition for scarce funding resources. Moreover, the end products—the projects—are usually better than when output measures such as the number who attended the programs are the only measures employed. The success, in terms of both educational value and numbers served, of programs planned and implemented using methodologies like PP&E is usually far greater because decisions affecting the services or programs are made at each step along the way, thereby assuring both fiscal and programmatic accountability and assuring the best possible products for the people. The best for the most is clearly a statement of accountability.

References

DeProspo, Ernest R. (1973). *A Program Planning and Training Manual, Draft III*. Unpublished manual issued by The College Entrance Examination Board. New York.

Gregorian, Vartan, & Schull, Diantha D. (1983). *Public Programs on "Printing and Censorship."* A proposal from the New York Public Library submitted to the National Endowment for the Humanities, Division of General Programs, Humanities Projects in Libraries.

National Foundation on the Arts and the Humanities. (1970). Act of 1965 (Public Law 209—89th Congress as amended through July 20, 1970. U.S.C. 951 *et seq.* Washington, DC: U. S. Government Printing Office.

9

Accountability in the Classroom

Charles Curran

College of Library and Information Science
University of South Carolina

In addition to being a pioneer researcher in the measurement of library operations, Ernest R. DeProspo was also a teacher—and a very good one. Once in his doctoral seminar on research methods, he expressed great interest in a point of view attributed to Abraham Kaplan by an anxious doctoral student who was grappling with one of that author's more obscure but thankfully less opaque pronouncements.

"Kaplan rejects the notion of the philosopher as a middleman," suggested the student.

The point had come from a Kaplan article that not even DeProspo had read and it fascinated him. Much to the student's relief and delight, his professor savored Kaplan's idea and appeared to want to talk about it. But the class time had expired and the concept was never pursued in seminar again, for the following week it was another student's turn to lead, and novice Ph.D. seekers sought to display their own insights into research methodology, not some rival's.

Now, 17 years later, as I turn my attention to the subject of accountability in the classroom and to the influence of Ernest R. DeProspo, I like to think that I may have some inkling as to why he also rejected the role of middleman in both his research and his teaching, and why he was so very accomplished at and passionate about both.

THE MIDDLEMAN

We know that a middleman is a second party who sells to a third party goods which have been manufactured, grown, or assembled by a first party. There can even be tiers of middlemen.

These middlepersons are the go-betweens, the suppliers who may relieve the party of the first part of some inventory, marketing, and sales responsibilities. They provide a valuable service in this complex world and lots of first parties use them. Lee Iacocca does, so do

Apple, Mary Kay, Jimmy Swaggart, and Thom McAn. Sometimes first parties downshift to a middle role. Middlepeople do not get to tinker much with with their suppliers' products or they find themselves without wheels, motherboards, lip gloss, salvation, or shoes—disenfranchised, in other words. Indeed, the Reverend Swaggart will testify to this.

RESEARCHERS AND TEACHERS IN THE MIDDLE?

Good researchers and teachers don't make good middlepersons, not in academic environments. The idea behind the *Research Agenda for the 1980s* (Cuadra, 1982) was to suggest to researchers that they ought to pursue the problems which others have identified as important. Good researchers like to pursue ideas which *they* identify as important. They don't like being in the middle. The *Agenda* fizzled.

Good teachers like to guide students through a process of identification and analysis that leads to insight. Good teachers really cannot adjust to someone else's lesson plan or syllabus. Mediocre ones can. Educational middlemen can teach from the text, from the notes—theirs or another's, and they can even teach *the* scientific method to novice conductors of inquiry. How accountable is that? Well, the answer may depend upon how *accountability* is defined or, more precisely, what it means.

ACCOUNTABILITY

Accountability is not even a buzz word anymore, which means that nobody bothers much to consider what it means. People just use it in whatever context seems appropriate to them. The word pops up in casual and serious conversations, contributing about as much structural integrity and meaning to a dialogue as a Slim Whitman yodel does to a lyric. Soon it will become like "hopefully," "in terms of," and "due to"—misused so often by so many people with excellent posture and good standing in the community that nobody will pay any attention to the meaning.

A definition of accountability might include some notion of responsibility to one's supervisor on whatever terms the supervisor sets forth and the supervisee agrees to. Accountability can be, therefore, whatever those in power to define and enforce accountability say it is. It may include the requirement that one owes the supervisor or employing agency an honest account of one's use of company time, money, and resources. Moreover, accountability may require one to spend company time, money, and resources in ways that benefit the company, as measured by some standards or norms established by the company. So in order to be fully accountable, one must earn and produce a record of honest, efficient service according to rules set up by one's employer.

Accountability, like Management by Objectives, POSDCORB, and other catchy terms, comes to educators and librarians via government. These terms all get filtered and purified in the process—changed to suit their new environments. In July of 1987 American television networks carried the Iran-Contra Hearings, proceedings which introduced many Americans to the concept of *plausible deniability*, referring to a situation wherein "it should be possible to carry out operations in a way that would enable the President to deny he knew about them" (Safire, 1978). Interestingly, these words are not descriptive of the mind set of a Ronald Reagan staff member but traceable to a position on "deniability" attributable circa 1978 to Jimmy Carter's National Security Adviser Zbigniew Brzezinski.

In his brilliant and witty political dictionary William Safire sketches the uses and meanings for accountability in politics, linking it with other political slanguage like *Oversight, Sign Off On*, and oxymorons such as *Waging Peace* (Safire, 1978).

When educators and library managers took hold of *Accountability*, they invested it with more benign connotations. And so for library managers *accountability* has come to be associated with being responsible for what happens when they spend public moneys, for establishing organizational goals and objectives, for rendering truthful evaluations of subordinates, and for reporting all this to boards, government agencies, funders and the public (Stueart & Eastlick, 1981).

So What? for Educators

How does any of this apply to the teacher of library and information science? Operationally, it can find expression in evaluation procedures designed to provide an account of a teacher's performance. Criteria are identified and defined, norms are established (or not established, as is sometimes the case with "Scholarship and Publication," where numbers and/or refereed status of journals are never weighted considerations), and a year's service is measured against objectives agreed upon for that period. The following criteria are frequently chosen:

Teaching Effectiveness
Research and Publication
College/University Service
Professional (Organizational) Activity
Community Service
Colleagial Support (Cooperating, helping fellows)

These criteria *work* to the extent that all concerned parties understand and agree upon what each term means, to the extent that the university acknowledges them as the indicators of accountability and accepts whatever has been declared to be the measure of excellence, and to the extent that the university rewards those teachers whom she judges accountable. With respect to teaching effectiveness, a teacher is *accountable*, therefore, if he gets high evaluations from students on the approved evaluation instruments.

Is that so? It is if we measure accountability for teaching effectiveness solely on the basis of an end-of-term instrument, frequently a series of forced choices presented to a group of students experiencing exam fatigue, an assortment of anxieties and incipient burnout.

MEASURING ACCOUNTABILITY

If we were to agree that accountability has something to do with effective performance and honest reporting, and that accountability is a good thing, we would still be faced with the problem of measuring it. Simplistic approaches like: *the measure of a reading teacher's effectiveness is how well Johnny scores on a standardized reading test* have a solid, bottom-line appeal. But such two-dimensional pronouncements do not explain outcomes in a multidimensional environment such as the classroom.

One who goes in search of better ways to define and measure accountability should adopt a more ecological approach to the problem. A systems point of view will enable him to examine the issue in a broader context. For example, viewing accountability as descriptive of a process will prevent one from falling into the trap of thinking that it is some quality that is capturable on an evaluation sheet, test score, or transcript, that it is locatable at a point on some linear landscape. Also, by viewing the issue of accountability as a *process* of becoming accountable, one is drawn to identify and describe inputs and outputs. Figure 9.1 displays this notion.

Figure 9.1 hardly makes the problem of describing accountability

Figure 9.1.   Inputs—Processes—Outputs.

Inputs	Processes	Outputs
Agency Support	Teaching & Research	Graduates
Salary	Instructing	Articles
Facilities	Mentoring	Books
Expectations	Counseling	Appearances
Allowances		
	Publishing	
Students		
Talents	Serving Professional Groups	
Aptitudes		
Ambitions		
Efforts		

an easy one, but it does display some of the variables that should be taken into consideration. Effective performance in the classroom is going to mean different things in different kinds of institutions. Their protestations notwithstanding, some research-oriented institutions tolerate poor teaching (even *no* teaching) by those whose research and publication activities enhance the reputations of the schools. At the other extreme, so-called *teaching* institutions, those which appear not to to emphasize and/or reward research and publication, may insist on excellence in the classroom. Between the poles there exist numerous variations on those themes. The kinds of support inputs provided by an institution are going to influence institutional expectations and institutional definitions of accountability. And there ought to be some congruity among support, expectation, definition, evaluation, and reward.

Figure 9.1 may suggest that students bring to the classroom differing talents, aptitudes, and ambitions. Is it not curious that in some of the very institutions in which insights about individual differences, cognitive maps, and innovative teaching are developed, the most mundane and vanilla teaching goes on and the most primitive of accountability measures are employed, both with students and with faculty?

How accountable should teachers be for the performance and attitudes of the very bright student or of the less bright student? Do admissions requirements bar the unqualified? May counseling activities weed out the few students who, although they possess the requisite academic skills, suffer from severe personality disorders? Have such persons been advised by kindly chaplains to seek low stress employment opportunities in librarianship or the macrame industry? Whatever the case, faculty are, and must be, responsible to their hiring agencies and to their students.

Figure 9.1 suggests that faculty demonstrate accountability by converting certain inputs to outputs via the processes of teaching, advising, publishing, and serving. In that faculty may have the choice in determining how they will teach, what they will study (depending upon the availability of funding, of course) and how they will publicize their findings, individual differences and preferences get considered.

"THE" MEASURE OF ACCOUNTABILITY

It's the output that gets "measured" in order to determine the extent of accountability. Do the graduates, in the process of their becoming graduates, give their teachers high marks? Do the authored books and articles exist in sufficient quantity? Pick a number, any number! None isn't enough; one hundred is a lot.

The major problem with the Inputs—Processes—Outputs figure is that it has more of the properties of a flow chart than of a real model. It is too abstract to be operational. While a judicious inspection of its ingredients can provide a more holistic view of the process of defining and assessing accountability, the figure falls far short of indicating ways to accomplish those tasks. Though it lacks prescriptive properties, it does display descriptive ones. And these may provide some helpful insights. For example, when the process of teaching in a professional school is placed in a broader context to include the environments in which graduates find employment, then the extent to which their educations prepared them for that employment ought to be a factor in determining the accountability of the educators. Since evaluations administered on the last day of class are hardly capable of describing any relationship between instruction and employment that has not yet begun, accountability can be associated with student perceptions of how well they were entertained for a semester or how well they were lectured at.

The point here is not to confuse education for the information professions with on-the-job training, nor to ignore the fact that the majority of students now enrolled in graduate programs in library and information science are part-time students holding full- or part-time jobs (Curran, 1987). These students, obviously, may be able to appreciate relationships between education and employment, relationships which are not apparent to their full-time, fresh-out-of-undergraduate school classmates.

Figure 9.1 can also remind us that in a philosophical or ethical sense, educators are accountable to a variety of people—to students, to institutions, to funding agencies, to colleagues, and to themselves. It implies that classroom teachers are accountable for taking an assortment of students who claim they want to work in the information professions from where they are to where they want to be. Such is not a job for middlemen. For middlemen can only be the agents through which students learn the enduring truths of the business, like 973 is the Dewey Number for American history, the index to the *World Almanac* is in the front, AACR2 comes after AACR, one byte equals eight bits (for now), and in a library that charges overdue fines of five cents per day the tab for a book that is three days late is fifteen cents (unless returned during a grace period).

Middlemen can parrot the pronouncements of the texts, distribute classification schedules and lists of recommended reference books, and score multiple guess tests, but they do not like to, nor can they:

1. Get students excited about the fact that libraries are unique institutions which provide a unique assortment of services
2. Explain to students about information, the only commodity that doesn't get used up when it is consumed
3. Involve students in the wondrous phenomenon that is information transfer
4. Convince students that their chief problems on the job will be people problems, not technical ones
5. Suggest to students that their survival may depend upon how well they understand the behavior of information and the behavior of people toward information
6. Give students a satisfactory experience with systematic problem solving and encourage their respect for and interest in the conduct of inquiry
7. Explore with students the notion that librarians and information agents have to check in with the outer environment in order to be good librarians and agents.

When they act upon inclinations that others do not have and explore insights which others do not see, researchers and teachers reject the role of middleperson. How *accountable* such people are is to a large extent dependent upon how useful their insights are, how much impact their research has upon the productive efforts of those who follow, and how well their influence has prepared their students to function after graduation.

ARE THESE THINGS MEASURABLE?

Will we ever be able to measure these things? Perhaps. Some people claim that in some cases we already can, asserting that citation counts are indicative of the influence of one writer upon other writers. Other people assert just as forcefully that such counts merely reflect the pathology of publish-or-perish hysteria, a syndrome which includes the bulimic response. According to them, the sociology of information transfer is hardly a manifestation of excellence or accountability.

Relating accountability in the classroom to performance on the job presents extremely difficult conceptual and methodological problems. How much of one's performance, for example, is attributable to talent and disposition, education before or after the MLS, the MLS program, individual teachers within that program, on-the-job training, or other factors? What are the relationships between type of specialty and classroom training? What about workers in alternative or nonlibrary occupations?

Unless *The* scientific method is discredited, or until the Aquarian Conspirators manage to convince us that there are reliable alternative ways to know, anecdotal evidence from the workplace is unlikely to replace the "hard" evidence produced by some evaluation procedures. Room must be made for reports from the field, however, for they can be truer indicators of accountability than other measures in use.

This writer is reminded of a letter he recently received from a former student he hadn't seen in 16 years. In it she referred to a professor she had encountered at library school, a teacher so inept that the students circulated a petition to have him removed. "I've always remembered what [so and so] said about [such and such], and I practice that every day in my work," wrote the ex-student, an extremely successful information professional in New York City. So much for real-time evaluation.

   Anecdotal!
   N of one!
   Unreliable, unsolicited personal testimony!

True, but how much more relevant to the concept of accountability is this letter than, say, the evaluations written after that professor's last class? How much more valid might the comment in the letter be?

If accountability shall continue to be defined as that which those empowered to require it say it is, then the question of how to measure it is of little practical significance. Those measures are in place. If a more holistic view of accountability were adopted, one that included some of the elements contained in or suggested by Figure 9.1, then the problem of measurement surfaces. Some things may defy measurement; others may simply be as yet unmeasured. Appreciating the difference is a must and it is not a job for a middleman.

To each of his classes in research methods Ernest R. DeProspo always managed to read a great verse he attributed to e. e. cummings. It was a condemnation of a real hammerer, an insensitive "Son of a bitch that would presume to measure springtime."[1] This lesson was not the admonition of a middleman, but the wise counsel of an original thinker and advocate of measurement who understood that if one passes out free hammers, potential takers will decide that lots of things need to be hammered, and if one develops easy-to-use measures, some people will decide to use them on everything.

It doesn't work that way.

REFERENCES

Cuadra Associates. (1982). *A library and information science research agenda for the 1980s. Summary Report*. Santa Monica: Cuadra Associates.

Curran, C. (1987). The distant learner as part-time learner. *Journal of Library and Information Science Education, 27*, 33–55.

Safire, W. (1978). *Safire's political dictionary; An enlarged, up-to-date edition of the new language of politics*. New York: Ballantine Books.

Stueart, R., & Eastlick, J. T. (1981). *Library Management* (2nd ed). Littleton, CO: Libraries Unlimited. (There is a 3rd edition of this title.)

---

[1] This writer ended his quest for the specific origin of the quoted lines after his search, that of his graduate assistant, and the investigation of several colleagues in the English Department, uncovered no exact reference.

10
Staff Development and Organizational Change

Barbara Williams Jenkins

Director, Miller F. Whittaker Library
South Carolina State College

THE WAY IT WAS

Staff development is not a new concept in libraries, but a new term in a changed library environment affected by internal and external technological, social, and political developments. Before the 1960s staff development in the information professions was generally considered to be synonymous with inservice education, and there was no comprehensive national emphasis as there is today (Stone, 1986). Generally, library management was documented by outstanding library managers such as Guy R. Lyle whose advice was respected by followers in all types of libraries and upon whom many librarians depended for their "continuing" education.

THE CHANGING ENVIRONMENT AND LIBRARIES

In the 1960s and 1970s the social climate became people-oriented, and the institution of the library began with new energy to focus services and programs on users. Libraries were advertised as information centers. Open stack systems proliferated. Computer systems moved in. Users were offered more choices than ever before. Technological enhancement changed the way information got organized and retrieved and increased the amounts of information to which users had access. Because of these developments staffs were also forced to change.

Like other institutions, libraries were undergoing organizational change. Management styles were shifting. Bureaucratic models gave way to participative ones. The changing social climate was characterized in part by new feelings of personal worth and the need to develop oneself more fully. Adults sought verbal and social skills, and they grew more comfortable in expressing their feelings about their professional and personal lives. They began to expect more from social institutions such as schools, colleges, and local and state governments, and they began to demand accountability from these institutions.

Librarians were included in this phenomenon, and they began to get asked in-depth questions about performance of staff, programs, services, and collections. To answer these questions staffs had to be trained to develop surveys, user studies, and performance measures. Some managers began to believe that the development and effective use of these tools was crucial for the survival of libraries.

TECHNOLOGICAL CHANGES

Most librarians agree that technology has had an astounding impact on the field. The computer and advanced systems have released librarians from many manual and mundane tasks like record keeping and filing. But more importantly, today sophisticated information retrieval systems assist librarians in providing users with the main product—information—in a matter of seconds. Technological systems permit the sharing of resources and information among libraries through giant networks like OCLC. Information retrieval systems, such as DIALOG and Bibliographic Retrieval Services (BRS), offer new and speedy approaches to librarians and other users. Integrated library systems, incorporated online access to catalogs, and the electronic library have changed the environment of the library and the roles of library staff. This change will continue.

With the changing organizational and technological environment of the library came the need to examine institutional and staff goals and objectives. Some observers believed a new kind of staff needed to emerge, along with redefined tasks and titles. In the early 1970s the model advanced by the Columbia University Plan enabled some librarians to effect such changes. Management Review and Analysis (MRAP) had such an impact, and there seems to be movement for change in the way departments such as cataloging and reference view and execute their functions. Questions surfaced about whether the library research related to organizational theory had any positive association with helping users (Howard, 1984).

ORGANIZATIONAL CHANGE AFFECTS STAFF DEVELOPMENT

The terms *efficiency* and *effectiveness* relate to staff development, just as they relate to efforts to describe quality programs. This writer's definition of staff development is as follows: It has to do with developing the worker's potential for providing improved services to clientele; it has to do with developing, promoting, and evaluating the integrating of organizational goals; it is developing self-esteem and striving for self-actualization; and it includes the continuous evaluation of self and of one's contributions to organizational growth.

The organizational environment, whether it be a library, school, hospital, or corporation, functions best when workers' basic needs are satisfied and when there is an integration of personal and organizational goals. The organizational environment grows and develops, and workers who have positive self-images and solid work skills can be part of this growth and development.

The right combination. Staff development occurs when there is a coalition of the individual and the organization, preparing both for the future and strengthening the capabilities of both. It is a process of fusion. Wise administrators do not overpower the organization with heavy-handed efforts to accomplish this fusion. Instead they make the effort to know and understand the behavior of people in the work environment, to identify their capabilities, to acknowledge their dreams and aspirations, and to link the right person with the right job.

The onslaught of change brings challenges to staff efficiency and effectiveness. Special staff development programs, aimed at arming employees and helping them cope with change, need to be designed. These programs can assure employees that:

1. Change need not threaten employee security.
2. Participation in meeting the challenge of change can improve organizational decision making and promote general well-being.
3. Trust and confidence can be maintained.
4. Communications can be open and productive.
5. Channels to and opportunities for personal development can be established. These include in-service training, workshops, conferences, classes, and degree programs.

Benefits. If such programs were instituted and maintained in libraries, then observers see a number of benefits for them:

1. The potential for cohesive efforts to work for the improvement of the total system.
2. The creation of programs with planned changes.
3. The development of mentors and role models.
4. The development of career plans.
5. The creation and utilization of research studies and findings.

6. The development of new models for improved library services and programs.

This writer is convinced, both by the findings of expert observers and by the experiences she has encountered, that solid staff development provides an agency with its best method for dealing with change in both external and internal environments and with its best chance at increasing organizational effectiveness.

Relationships. Theorists and model builders such as Maslow, Likert, Argyris, and McGregor have supplied many useful insights for managers and administrators, to whom they issue reminders about how the human condition affects organizational behavior. They prepare planners to consider societal changes and their impact on behavior in the workplace. Their findings should prompt planners of staff development to include attention to human relations, the individual personality, the nature of organizations, and the development of relationships within the organizations. Related to these are perceptions of oneself, work and work environment; job satisfaction; organization for effective performance; and the maintenance of the proper organizational climate—one conducive to the development of trust and respect.

STAFF DEVELOPMENT IN THE PROFESSION

In the past 20 years staff development programs in libraries have multiplied, mostly because of the galloping changes occurring in both the external and internal environments of libraries and the perceived need to understand and deal with those changes.

The Continuing Library Education Network and Exchange (CLENE) was established to promote this cause and to alert information professionals about available programs of continuing education. Library schools, library associations, and library consultants got into the act, and today the library literature is abundant with announcements for workshops, seminars, and conferences designed to meet the specific needs of information workers to update and expand their skills. *American Libraries* has offered a course by mail.

Staff development gains increasing mention in the literature. Some library standards advocate staff development programs. The Systems and Procedures Exchange Center designed SPEC kits on staff and professional development for academic libraries (Association, 1981).

Also, the Staff Development Committee of the Personnel Administration section of the ALA Library Administration and Management Association (LAMA) published *Staff Development in Libraries Bibliography* which identified some of the major topics of concern for continuing education: Affirmative Action, Career Development, Communication, Motivation, Orientation, Performance Appraisal, Stress, Supervision, and Management. It is instructive to note the shift in focus in the 1983 bibliography which:

> emphasizes staff development as practiced by managers and supervisors; this is to be distinguished from 'continuing education' which is often provided by outside agencies and not integrated into the operating context. Staff development activities focus on providing staff with knowledge and skills directly related to their job responsibilities while continuing education activities focus upon the needs of the individual rather than the needs of the organization. (American Library Association, 1983, p. 1)

A review of the 1982 SPEC kit on Professional Development in ARL libraries reveals that:

> Although participation in professional development activities continues to depend heavily upon personal initiative, current evidence indicates that libraries and their parent institutions are assuming greater responsibility for planning, encouraging and facilitating programs. Organizational and operational changes, as well as the growing pressure to improve production, are primarily responsible for libraries' increased interest in expanding staff knowledge and skills. (Association, 1981, p. 1–1)

DO STAFF DEVELOPMENT PROGRAMS MAKE A DIFFERENCE?

Much has been written in the last two decades about staff development, and the volume seems to parallel the interest. Some of the literature describes the state of the art: Most of it is anecdotal, but several research studies have been conducted and reported.

Burlingame and Woods (1980) conducted a survey to discover what academic libraries were doing with staff development programs. Howard (1984) reports studies by Kaser, Breiting, Dorey, and Sockbesoh. There were some common findings which show agency support for travel to continuing education events, the practice of granting flex-time schedules for those who wish to participate in continuing education, and the absence of funds set aside for staff development programs. In-house programs appear to be a favored recommendation, and there appears to be evidence that some libraries are providing these kinds of staff development opportunities, especially in networking and management.

Swisher, Smith, and Boyer (1983) report increasing proportions of librarian participation in continuing education opportunities, especially academic courses.

Kohl's (1983) study reported preferences with respect to continuing education and staff development opportunities. Professional literature was the preferred locus. Local and regional workshops scored well. In terms of subject preference, it seems that participants viewed the literature and the tailored workshop favorably, believing that each can be designed for local applications. Preference for the *practical* is clear.

Boyer and Theimer (1975) reported some limited opportunities for library support staff development; so did the Olsgaards (1981). The majority of libraries reported no formal inservice programs for support staff. These studies focused primarily upon academic libraries. Monroe (1976) surveyed public libraries and found evidence of training for support staff in the following subject areas: community contacts, community study, human relations, group process, and community development. The majority expression seemed to be for more training in the areas of human relations and group process.

Institutional requirements in academic environments call for attendance at and participation in professional meetings and workshops, and this may account for what appears to be a greater volume of staff development activity in these organizations.

Whether participants and sponsors find these activities "useful" because they, in fact, are "useful" or because they provide a way for individuals to satisfy expectations of employers is a question that is not squarely addressed by the majority of studies conducted to date.

Yes, staff development programs make a difference. A difference in *what* remains substantially undiscovered.

SOME ISSUES; SOME "WHAT" TO INVESTIGATE

The entry level degree. With respect to the development of information professionals, there are some issues that need to be addressed. One has to do with education and focuses upon ALA endorsement of the master's degree as the entry requirement. "Entry requirements" for many positions, however, as indicated by ads for those posts, include the doctorate as the required educational qualification. Library educators and library administrators have ranked highly the acquisition of that degree. Indeed, the doctoral production of the 1970s was 10 times that of the 1950s or 1960s (Williamson, 1986).

The Olsgaards (1981) have shown the rising educational requirements for college library directors in their survey of job listings. Swisher, Smith, and Boyer (1983) compared 1973 and 1978 surveys of Association of College and Research Libraries members and found that the number of doctorates and doctoral students had more than doubled in the later period.

Perhaps ALA should reconsider its position based upon these developments. In many cases the job market belies the claim that the master's degree is the entrance and exit degree. ALA might give needed emphasis on the acquisition of specialist or doctoral degree as a personal development goal. As it now stands, the individual is often caught between the requirements of the hiring institution and the pronouncements of the professional organization.

Certification. Another issue is national certification. This idea has been proposed on numerous occasions. A national certification requirement could encourage librarians to become accountable for keeping up with current developments, learning new techniques and improving competencies. Stone (1986) once observed that the library degree has a short half-life. There is current reason to believe her forecast is too generous with respect to how long such a degree can avoid obsolescence.

Other professions—those of law, medicine, dentistry and pharmacy—require their memberships to continue their education for licensing purposes. Education professions are moving toward competency-based certification. These professional groups link the acquisition of current training with accountability. So should the information professions. There seems to be a mood in the country, an inclination to want to hold each other accountable for performance. So that their craft may endure, and so that they might succeed as individual practitioners, librarians should give serious thought to acquiring, and acquiring anew, the competencies required for practice in the Information Age and to establishing national certification.

The professional schools and the several professional associations should cooperate to rethink licensing and to provide the opportunities for certification and recertification.

Competencies. A related issue that could, if it were to be resolved, help planners develop licensing criteria is the establishment of competencies for library and information professionals. This is a real stumbling block, however, for while lists of such competencies enjoy considerable notoriety, few, except for several that concern a single segment of the information professions, have gained favorable notice. In the abstract it has not been difficult to link the concepts of competency and accountability, but efforts to draw lists have fallen short of achieving real-world linkage.

CHALLENGES TO THE FUTURE
OF STAFF DEVELOPMENT PROGRAMS

Maintaining, monitoring, and evaluating staff development programs are chief responsibilities for library administrators. A related and critical need is for the hiring of individuals who are prepared and disposed to take advantage of continuing education. Administrators look for such persons of "good fit." So what a person brings to the organization in the way of qualifications and attitudes is likely to determine how he views opportunities to work for program goals and personal goals as well. Being able to spot these qualities in applicants is a crucial skill for administrators.

It might be that the obligation to prepare information professionals who can be consumers of continuing education, productive promoters of organizational aims, and change agents can be shared by a triangle of professionals: teachers, researchers, and the workers themselves. Cooperatively, they could add much to staff development programs. Perhaps they could provide the needed blend of theory and practice which appears to be so elusive.

There is a role to play for a foundation here, perhaps a think tank kind of operation whose purpose will be to spot trends, consider applications, review policies, and study the future. This foundation could supply answers to questions like: What kind of professional is needed now and in the future? What kinds of training would be most useful in which kinds of staff development programs?

How we tackle the questions related to accountability and staff development may determine whether *we* continue to be the ones to ask the questions.

REFERENCES

American Library Association. Library Administration and Management Association. (1983). *Staff development in libraries bibliography*. Chicago: American Library Association.
Association of Research Libraries, Systems and Procedures Exchange Center,

SPEC Flyer/Kit. (1981). *Staff development*. Washington, DC: Association of Research Libraries.

Boyer, L., & Theimer, W. C. (1975). The use and training of non-professional personnel at reference desks at selected college and university libraries. *College and University Libraries, 36*, 193–200.

Burlingame, D., & Woods, J. (1980). Staff development and continuing education in the university library setting. *Journal of Library Automation, 1*, 41–46.

Howard, H. (1984). Organization theory and its application to research in librarianship. *Library Trends, 32*, 477–493.

Kohl, D. (1983). Circulation professionals: Management information needs and attitudes. *RQ, 23*, 81–86.

Monroe, Margaret. (1976). Community development as a mode of community analysis. *Library Trends, 24*, 497–514.

Olsgaard, John, & Olsgaard, Jane. (1981). Post MLS educational requirements for academic librarians. *College and Research Libraries, 42*, 224–228.

Swisher, Robert, Smith, Peggy, & Boyer, Calvin. (1983). Educational change among ACRL academic librarians. *Library and Information Science Research, 5*, 192–205.

Stone, E. (1986). Growth of continuing education. *Library Trends, 34*, 489–513.

Williamson, W. L. (1986). A century of students. *Library Trends, 34*, 433–449.

11

Applying Nontraditional Perspectives to Traditional Library Research: Critical Theory as Method

Alan R. Samuels

School of Library and Information Science
University of Missouri—Columbia

INTRODUCTION

> Many practical people believe that theory gets in the way of practice and that, by and large, theorizing is a waste of time. But there is a great fallacy in this way of thinking. For in recognizing how taken for granted images or metaphors shape understanding and action, we are recognizing the role of theory. Our images or metaphors are theories or conceptual frameworks. Practice is never theory free, for it is always guided by an image of what one is trying to do. The real issue is whether or not we are aware of theory guiding our action. (Morgan, 1986, p. 336)

The ideas represented by the above quotation reflect a picture of Ernest DeProspo's thinking that is often not recognized by those who did not work with him on a day-to-day basis. DeProspo is usually thought of as one solely interested in quantification and mensuration. But in his work with students he was deeply concerned with concept and theory. The views presented in this chapter, I hope, will help provide some understanding of the multifaceted features of DeProspo's thinking.

The immediate purpose of this chapter is to discuss several new perspectives familiar to sociological researchers and to examine their potential usefulness in clarifying library and information-oriented problems, in particular, those of planning. Major focus is placed on Critical Theory since, as a sort of "meta-theory," it represents the type of evaluation with which DeProspo was most concerned. Neither a treatise on methodology nor an exhaustive recitation of problems, it gives instead a brief glance at new directions in theory that are already driving practice in several areas of library and information-related study.[1]

A CHANGE OF EMPHASIS

A Problem

At the present time library and information science research appears to be defined by the way it is taught. If this is axiomatic, then such research always will be quantitative (Daniel, 1987), lacking in theoretical backing, and avoiding any philosophical intent. The discipline favors problem-oriented, action research rather than the more basic type that is less amenable to instantaneous use. Sufficient evidence of this can be found in the commonalty of textbooks in this area, all of which tend to cover the same quantitative ground in one way or another, occasionally dealing with qualitative research as an aside.[2]

The conduct of inquiry in library and information studies depends in large part on the definition of terms. There is no consensus on definitions, nor is there any agreement on whether library science or information studies are human or natural sciences (or "sciences" at all). Coming to some sort of common understanding on working definitions of these two areas of study is significant since, practically speaking, methodology follows accepted research conventions of the discipline in which lies the locus of the problem to be investigated. For the purposes of this paper, "library and information studies" are considered as part of the human sciences oriented toward attributing meaning to observed phenomena. Thematic throughout is the notion that "meaning" is synonymous with "understanding." As such, the focus of human sciences research is on the creation of understanding through the interaction of human agents and their environments.

---

[1] See Chatman, Elfreda A. (1985). Information, Mass Media Use and the Working Poor. *Library and Information Science Review, 7,* 97–113, and Chatman, Elfreda A. (1987). The Information World of the Low Skilled Workers. *Library and Information Science Review, 9,* 265–283. Her avowed purpose is to investigate information diffusion theory, but her work is primarily ethnomethodological. As such it is an excellent example of the practical application of Critical Theory.

[2] Probably the most widely used text is Busha, Charles H., & Harter, Stephen P. (1980). *Research Methods in Librarianship: Techniques and Interpretation.* New York: Academic Press. Only about one quarter of the book is given over to qualitative methods.

Some Transition

In recent years library research has begun to undergo transition. It has begun to leave its logical positivistic grounding in order to investigate and use perspectives derived from other disciplines in an integrative way that applies new methods to traditional library-related problems.

Traditional problems are those questions which have been subjected to frequent investigation over a period of time. The most obvious of these is termed "user studies," a catch-all phrase that includes questions such as: What is a "library user?" Other more recent examples are "performance measures" and "planning." Yet another is "catalog use," whether that catalog is the traditional kind or the more recent online version. Marchant and Smith (1982) have identified a number of areas that practitioners consider to be of increasing importance. While many of these are technology-oriented, some high-priority items are cognitive in nature and deal with a librarian's ability to better understand the political and social environment within which the library functions. Several common threads run throughout these problems:

1. They are nearly all competency-based.
2. They are quantitatively oriented.
3. They have been subjected to multiple investigations using traditional methods.

Qualitative and Quantitative

"Traditional methods" are those *techniques* which have been used to gather data that can contribute to finding solutions for traditional problems. *Methodology*, on the other hand, refers to the study of those techniques. In recent years quantitative methods in library science research have come under increasing fire because of their propensity to rule out results that are not subject to traditional criteria of verification such as those linked with direct, value-neutral, observation. While new to the library field, research dealing with the process of *understanding* is gradually becoming at least as important as research dealing with *explanation* and *description*. For some time now this has been among the central concerns of sociological and phenomenological research.

That research concerned with "understanding" is usually referred to as "qualitative." The areas with which qualitative research is concerned are the "human sciences," those sciences concerned with human experiences, perceptions, beliefs, and values.[3] Human science research:

> can be defined as a systematic exploration and understanding of meaning, behavior, and interaction in the context of human experience. It represents an umbrellalike unity across different disciplines . . . . What unites the group is the recognition that human existence needs to be approached in its own terms rather than on conceptual foundations borrowed from the natural sciences. (Barrell, 1987, p. 452)

Thus human science research encompasses a wide variety of study areas normally thought of as discrete from one another.

Human science research can be further distinguished by five elements:

1. PURPOSE—to obtain a more thorough understanding of human experience.
2. METHODOLOGY—characterized by the suspension of conceptual presuppositions in order to describe and understand meanings fully as they are immediately given in experience.
3. QUESTIONS—formulated in such a way as to address human experience as it is lived.
4. DATA COLLECTION—includes descriptions of situations lived by the researcher or other subjects considered as valid sources of information from which to reach an understanding of human experience.
5. DATA ANALYSIS—considered a method through which the meanings implicit in human experience are brought into clearer focus (Barrell, 1987).

---

[3] These are generally referred to in the literature as "Geisteswissenshaften," a term variously translated as "human sciences" or simply as the "humanities." The use of the term is not an exercise in academic obscurity but rather reflects the notion that components of the Geisteswissenshaften range from the philosophic to the sociological and psychological as opposed to the tripartite division of "philosophical, sociological, and natural" sciences. For an excellent and easily accessible discussion of the meaning, origin, and use of Geisteswissenshaften see Polkinghorne, Donald (1983). *Methodology for the Human Sciences: Systems of Inquiry.* Albany: State University of New York.

DIFFICULTIES OF CURRENT LIBRARY RESEARCH

Harris (1986) has noted that the present ideology of library research relies almost totally on a positivist epistemology. Among the most significant reasons for this is intellectual isolation. As Harris puts it in a review of the 1984 issue of *Library Trends* devoted to research (1984, p. 109), "a reading of this volume leads one to the unblinkable conclusion that we have deliberately committed an act of collective intellectual impoverishment." Harris then goes on to list several reasons for this "impoverishment." Among these are excessive selectivism of *what* to research as well as strict adherence to a conservative viewpoint that "has severely limited the range of questions that can be investigated, and has rigidly defined the characteristics of a good answer. Over the years this work has become increasingly sophisticated: it is also increasingly trivial" (Harris, 1984, p. 109).

In this he reflects a similar view held at various times by Pierce Butler and Jesse Shera. More than half a century ago, Butler noted the librarian's lack of interest in "the theoretical aspects of his profession . . . . The librarian apparently stands alone in the simplicity of his pragmatism; a rationalization of each immediate technical process by itself seems to satisfy his intellectual interest" (Butler, 1933, pp. xi-xii).

Shera (1972) continually argued for an interdisciplinary research orientation, especially with those disciplines that themselves are not formalized. In another context, Shera (1970, p. 158) was far less charitable to library researchers and indicted them for excessive concern with an almost medieval scholasticism that causes them to "fritter away their energies on infinitesimal and insignificant problems simply because they have been done, let us be frank about it, by infinitesimal and insignificant minds." In general, most critics of library and information science research are stressing the importance of a less positivistic approach to problem solving through an understanding of the symbolic world within which librarians function (Wright, 1986).

ALTERNATIVES

Typical of research dealing with "understanding" are those projects concerned with the experiences of human beings within their own "lifeworlds." Each individual, group, or society inhabits a certain "lifeworld" within which there is a sense of shared beliefs, values, and activities. A "lifeworld" can be extended or contracted depending upon the criteria that distinguishes it.[4] Each lifeworld has embedded within it the means of effectuating rational discourse leading to mutual understanding. In this it differs substantially from similar environmental metaphors such as Kurt Lewin's (1935) force field in which an individual is impelled toward certain actions by "driving" or "restraining" forces. Additional augmentation of the lifeworld inhabitants expands, enabling new developments to be recognized and discussed in terms of their contribution to emancipatory discourse. A good example of a Critical Theory perspective is the use (and misuse) of the computer in society. "The computer" can be viewed as either arbiter or helper. As "helper" the computer releases an individual or society from excessive mechanistic thought, as "arbiter" the computer produces results that are the *movers* of thought. In the first case technology represented by the computer contributes to mutual understanding, in the second it substitutes for it.[5]

Examination of the interaction of human agent and lifeworld can be accomplished by using one or more of several different perspectives. Among these are Critical Theory, Hermeneutics, and ethnomethodology, each of which bears a strong resemblance to the other. Interestingly enough, all have been used in library research though rarely recognized as such. In this paper I will focus on Critical Theory, not because it is necessarily the most important of these perspectives, but because it appears to be the one that offers the most hope for breaking down the paradigmatic cage that encloses much of what we do in research.

CRITICAL THEORY

Critical Theory submits commonly accepted assumptions and law-like propositions to logical and dialectical analysis in order to discover potential sources of distortions, gaps, or inadequate interpretations. Critical Theories aim first at understanding alternative or hidden explanations of visible or spoken phenomena in order to achieve emancipation from false assumptions and, as a consequence, from poten-

---

[4] For example, within the narrow world of the reference transaction there are usually two inhabitants of that "lifeworld," the librarian and the patron. By adding the sources for a library patron's query (the reference collection), the horizon of the original lifeworld of the inhabitants is extended.

[5] For a sustained example of "old style" Critical Theory in librarianship see Harris, Michael H. (1986). State, Class, and Cultural Reproduction: Toward a Theory of Library Service in the United States. In Wesley Simonton (Ed.), *Advances in Librarianship* (Vol. 14, pp. 211–251). New York: Academic Press.

tially harmful ways of acting, thus "making agents aware of hidden coercion, thereby freeing them from that coercion and putting them in a position to determine where their true interests lie" (Geuss, 1981, p. 55). Originally developed as a means of rehabilitating orthodox Marxist thought in a society that did not develop as Marx envisioned, Critical Theory espoused a meta-evaluative view of normative theory in an attempt to draw out possible inconsistencies in the latter.

Critical Theory has been characterized by an attempt to identify those societal forces that, through their emphasis on reproduction of normative modes of viewing the world, prevented disruption of the existing order. "Order" was used as a "repressive harmony" that prevented emancipation and progress by rejecting the need to problematize the predominant assumptions of society. In other words, Critical Theory postulated a "silent majority" whose voice is stilled by dominating and repressive mechanisms of society.

In this mode Critical Theory rejected any attempts to separate observable "fact" from the wider society in which that "fact" is embedded. Critical Theory rejects the positivistic notion of the value neutrality of objects of research as well as of the researchers themselves (Giroux, 1983).

Among American scholars, Critical Theory has become particularly influential in education. Perhaps the main proponent of a Critical Theory of Education in America is Henry Giroux. According to Giroux, three elements characterized the first phase of Critical Theory. The first of these was the necessity to understand the relationships that exist between the "particular and the whole, the specific and the universal. This position appears in direct contradiction to the empiricist claim that theory is primarily a matter of classifying and arranging facts" (Giroux, 1983, p. 17). A second requirement of Critical Theory is a clear recognition that all theory is value-laden and represents some set of interests by its proponents. By problematizing theory through removal of its law-like appearance, the Critical Theorist is able to question basic assumptions on which theory rests. If these basic assumptions continue to appear "true" after such questioning, they are further validated.

Finally, Critical Theory exhibits what Giroux calls an "unmasking function." It serves to promote a dialectical examination of its own validity as this validity relates to historical and social realities. As such, Critical Theory is "political" in that it seeks to encourage debate and dissent which, through synthesis (the dialectical process), produces a more holistic understanding of phenomena under study as representing both overt and hidden interests of social actors. In short, Critical Theory reveals the hidden agendas of societal institutions, synthesizes them with empirical research, and produces a more meaningful representation of the events it is describing.

PHASE 1

The first phase of modern Critical Theory espoused by theorists such as Max Horkheimer, Theodor Adorno, and Herbert Marcuse took as its main theme the reformulation of orthodox Marxism into a more general framework that could account for the failure of Marx's predicted apocalyptic conflict between capital and labor. Modern Critical Theory was reinforced by scholars whose intellectual growth took place during the decades coinciding with and following the worst episodes of the cold war era. Until recently, allegiance to earlier Neo-Marxian Critical Theory was emphasized, leading to a dreamlike historical reflection rather than an action program for change (Held, 1980; O'Neill, 1976; Sabia & Wallulis, 1983; Tar, 1977). At present, however, Critical Theory has regained some of its former vigor. It has become a program for action.

PHASE 2

The second and continuing phase is concerned with that program for action which replaced pure critique. Foremost among modern Critical Theorists is the German scholar Jürgen Habermas, whose voluminous writings since the early 1960s have had an enormous influence on both European and American philosophers and, more importantly, on social thought (McCarthy, 1978; Roderick, 1986). It is neither possible nor desirable to recapitulate the many themes of Habermas in this paper. However, some themes are worth noting, in particular Habermas' notion of "communicative competence," an expression of the predominant focus among sociologists and philosophers over the last few decades on analysis of language as a way of understanding how meaning is attributed to actions and symbols in the lifeworld, apparently something that has completely escaped the notice of librarians. Because the idea of communicative competence has such important implications for librarians (in the reference process, for example) it is worth looking at, however briefly.

Habermas' recent work deals extensively with the problems of communication, not in a methodological sense but rather as a means whereby individuals can obtain a common understanding of the world around them (the "lifeworld") as well as of each other. In order to emphasize this, Habermas postulates that mutual comprehension among individuals and the elements of society is achieved through communicative competence. In this he reflects the predominant philosophical and social issue of modern times, the nature of language as an expression of social action. In other words, actors in a particular lifeworld express their understanding of normative behavior through speech acts. A "speech act" is any symbolic expression of meaning. It can be verbal or nonverbal, directly understandable or evocative of a corresponding speech act by others. Speech acts can be viewed at many different levels. At the lowest level, a speech act is any utterance which is intelligible only within a specific context. Moving up the chain of complexity requires gradual development of linguistic competence through the combination of individual speech acts according to a presupposed grammar. That is how language comes about, through an intersubjective agreement by members of a particular lifeworld that *this* is the meaning of a collection of speech acts in a particular order, such as in a "sentence." Emancipation from dominating elements of the lifeworld, whether institutionalized or personalized, comes about through mutual understanding of these elements through discourse. Discourse is only possible through the achievement of communicative competence by actors in the lifeworld.

"*Communicative* competence is not just a matter of being able to produce grammatical sentences. In speaking we relate to the world about us, to other subjects, to our own intentions, feelings, and desires" (Habermas, 1981). In the process of discourse various claims are made by "listener" and "receiver" in order to achieve a measure of intersubjective agreement. This intersubjective agreement among participant actors in turn creates additional discourse that continually tests the truth and validity of that agreement. If, through dialectical interaction of language, change is deemed necessary in the structure of the lifeworld, argumentative discourse takes place, resulting in the restructuring of that lifeworld and a new set of intersubjective agreements. Thus change is always occurring through the mechanism of dialectics, thesis-antithesis-synthesis.

Dialectical discourse is based upon the willingness of participants to recognize distortions in communication. According to Benson:

> The dialectical method locates contradictions in social organizations rather than in the confrontation between people and their social arrangements. The arrangements consist of people acting in certain ways, carrying out certain practices. Contradictions are then confrontations between opposing or incompatible ways of arranging social life. The analytical task is to identify the social conjunctures, the combinations of social forces that make change possible or probable. This

knowledge may serve an emancipatory function, allowing people to see through the ideological covering of the social order and to understand crisis and potentialities for action. People may then act concertedly to contradict the limits of the social order. (Benson, 1983, p. 333)

Central to Habermas' perception of validity is his description of communication as a set of "speech acts." Each speech act makes certain claims, or demands, on the receiver. It is the need to accept or reject these claims through clarification that promotes dialogue and, ultimately, change. Once change takes place, the process is repeated as emerging contingencies in the lifeworld "reset" the boundaries within which social and communicative activity is carried out.

Habermas contends that in any dialogue speakers make four claims that "validate" what a particular speaker says. These are assumptions that, in an ideal situation, need to be accepted intersubjectively by inhabitants of particular lifeworlds. The validity claims are:

1. Comprehensibility, or the linguistic correctness of the speech act.
2. Truth, the speech act is grounded in some commonly understood referent.
3. Rightness, the speech act is appropriate for the situation.
4. Sincerity, the speech act is not deliberately distorted (Roderick, 1986, p. 89).

These validity claims determine whether or not a satisfactory understanding between speakers has occurred. What is "critical" about this type of validity is its amenability to contestation, to identifying and correcting mistakes. One learns from mistakes dealt with in such a manner.

Habermas denotes the "ideal speech situation" as identifiable by adequate satisfaction of each of the four validity claims. Achieving complete validation is an abstraction, similar to Abraham Maslow's "self-actualization," that Habermas has not yet converted into a specific plan for action. Nevertheless, several scholars have attempted this. The applications for Critical Theory that have been suggested are in those areas with which Ernest DeProspo was most concerned and to which current library energy is directed.

CRITICAL THEORY AND PLANNING

DeProspo often noted that planning, even at its best, is a messy business. Although his *Program Planning and Evaluation* (PP&E) was among the earliest planning efforts to take a sustained look at output measures, DeProspo always understood that differences in communities, clients, and populations made absolute and immutable prescriptions for planning impossible. In this he reflected a Critical Theory perspective on planning. That is, he recognized the potential distortions and misinterpretations that could result from inadequate understanding of what the planning process was all about.

In library circles today, "planning" is either abstract or prescriptive. There appears little middle ground that allows a conceptual grasp of planning to be converted into what Cris Argyris (1985) calls action science, a highly pragmatic effort to understand how individuals in particular lifeworlds design and implement activities. There are, to be sure, quite detailed descriptions of "the planning process." For example, the *Planning & Role Setting for Public Libraries* and its accompanying *Output Measures for Public Libraries* are meticulous prescriptions of how to plan, at least from the Public Library Association's point of view. A few parts of the PLA's planning process are examples of applying a critical perspective (i.e., Critical Theory). In the main, however, the document is not particularly different in basic concept from other planning efforts. In a metaphoric sense, the *Planning & Role Setting for Public Libraries* sets forth a mechanistic rather than organic set of rules that, if followed sequentially, may produce a coherent set of documents, in other words a "plan." From a Critical Theory point of view, PLA's planning process may seem to some as presenting a monolithic set of prescriptive communication rules and techniques. Interestingly, published critical comment and apologies, both, seem to ignore the library client's perspective (Rubin, 1986; D'Elia, 1988; Van House, 1985). Though his is a slightly irreverent comment upon the published reaction to PLA planning processes, Curran (1988) does address the issue from the user's perspective.

Using the Habermas formulation of Critical Theory planning results in a model of a different shape. John Forester (1985) has noted that planning cannot be purely empirical or normative because few lifeworld situations can be described as such. Utilizing a Critical Theory perspective, that is, systematically looking for possible barriers to communicative understanding, the researcher can help actors in the planning process anticipate and correct for potential obstacles that can retard the progress from planning to action. Critical Theorists look for those things that may cause resentment and mistrust of planners, that unintentionally produce counterproductive distortions of what planners want to accomplish.

Forester points out that planners need to provide *enabling* mechanisms that encourage mutual understanding among all participants. These enabling mechanisms are the norms of pragmatic communica-

tion and include avoidance of deliberate jargon or shamanistic mysti-
fication. To accomplish this, Forester suggests that those responsible
for planning consider the entire process as problematic, as open to
question and debate.

This is part of what PLA calls "planning to plan." However, the
description of this stage of planning appears to lack any real emphasis on discovering characteristic ways in which people view their own
lifeworlds rather than those of the library. Written forms and sequen-
tial steps are substituted for developing a planning culture with its
emphasis on understanding characteristic rituals and beliefs as well
as the linguistic competency and comprehensibility of actors in the
planning play (McClure, 1987; Samuels, 1982). Forester concludes
his analysis by suggesting that careful analysis of how communication operates within the planning process will prevent *systematic* distortion of such communication. He identifies several Critical Theory
strategies to facilitate the planning process; translation of specialized
discourse (jargon) into practical, ordinary language, identification of
potential types of disabling communicative speech acts (e.g., nonverbal negations of verbal suggestions), and clarification of the planner's
role as one who perpetuates or corrects communicative distortion.

In another context, Forester (1983) develops a specific method for
using Critical Theory as organizational analysis. Here he notes that:

> when organizations or polities are structured so that their members
> have no protected recourse to checking the truth, legitimacy, sincerity,
> or clarity claims made on them by established structures of authority
> and production, we may find conditions of dogmatism rather than of
> social learning, tyranny rather than authority, manipulation rather than
> cooperation, and distortion rather than sensitivity. (p. 242)

Forester is stressing the tendency of organizations to *replicate* and
reproduce the accepted norms and activities of organizational planning, however bizarre they may seem.

In order for planning to resist distortion, Mason and Mitroff (1981,
p. 10) suggest a dialectical Critical Theory that *deliberately* invokes
the process of thesis-antithesis-synthesis. Mason and Mitroff identify
what they call "wicked problems," problems that are complicated,
ambiguous, likely to cause conflict and anxiety among organizational
members, and the possibility of social pressures that mitigate against
unencumbered discourse. They suggest that "dialectics and argu-
mentation are methods of *systematizing* doubt" (p. 13) and, in so
doing, identifying needed information and communicative perspec-

tives that provide corrective synthesis through intersubjective discussion and agreement.

Critical Theory used in this manner has many benefits for planners. To begin with, it requires much broader participation by affected parties, directly or indirectly, in the policy-making process. Secondly, it requires that policy making be based on a wide spectrum of information gathered from a larger number of sources. Mason and Mitroff suggest a specific Critical Theory methodology for accomplishing the goal of dialectical planning called SAST (Strategic Assumption Surfacing Techniques). The SAST program requires that several different groups—groups that represent the thesis-antithesis-synthesis dialectical mode—be designated from those involved in the planning process. Each group then engages in dialectical debate in which "a situation is examined systematically and logically from two or more points of view" (Mason & Mitroff, 1981, p. 50). Finally, the authors describe several case studies in which the SAST method has been applied successfully.

The relevance of Critical Theory to public planning is made even clearer by Kemp. Applying Habermas' ideas of communicative competence to public hearings, Kemp argues that participants must be constantly on guard against communicative distortion. "Such groups as political activists, environmentalists, and political scientists should beware of the scientization of politics and attempts to depoliticize the public sphere through such means as mystifying terminology, bureaucratic rules, and the distortion of communication" (Kemp, 1985, p. 198). Kemp goes on to discuss several potential sources of communicative distortion that may be hidden, unrecognized, or very visible.

Critical Theory has been directly applied to information needs by Luke and White (1985). The authors emphasize the importance of language as carriers of information. The greater the distortion of communication through use of excessive jargon in place of ordinary language, the less freely and comprehensiby information will be communicated. This is especially true when that information being conveyed from members of one lifeworld to members of another. Here the major problems are those of different and sometimes diametrically opposed symbolic referents. To put it simply, the transfer of information is a communication problem, to be resolved through communication, either through linguistics, or through grammatical, semantic, or semeiotic means. Each participant in the communication process is accountable for his or her speech acts. Only through mutual discourse can the incommensurability of different social environments be alleviated.

THE UTILITY OF CRITICAL THEORY

This chapter can only convey a very small part of the richness of nontraditional methods that await the discovery of library and information researchers. The task will be difficult. New vocabularies will have to be learned. Above all, those who wish to investigate what has become traditional in the social and human sciences must adopt a methodological curiosity, an interest in theory, and a willingness to speculate on possible implications of what is examined. On the other hand, researchers must not forget the mundane in pursuit of the ethereal. Agassi brings this point home with force. In warning against the tendency to obscure rather than to clarify, Agassi writes, "When you read a paper or an essay or a tome of Martin Heidegger, you do not comprehend it and suspect that it is very deep indeed, and so you are prepared to admire it, to believe your friend's assurance that it is admirable" (Agassi, 1979, p. 211).

The best guidebooks to this relatively untraveled terrain are the works of Gareth Morgan that have been frequently alluded to in this paper. Morgan's *Beyond Method* (1983) describes no less than 23 different qualitative strategies for conducting research. His goal was to engender a more reflective social science.

> A knowledge of technique needs to be complemented by an appreciation of the nature of research as a distinctively human process through which researchers *make* knowledge. Such appreciation stands in contrast to the more common view of research as a neutral, technical process through which researchers simply reveal or discover knowledge. (p. 7)

Metaphor, or analogous views of lifeworlds, have also been treated by Morgan (1986) in his *Images of Organization*. In a remarkable tour de force the author views organizations from many different perspectives: as "psychic prisons, political systems, instruments of domination" and others. Each metaphor reveals more about the true nature of its subject, not because each is viewed alone but rather as a grand synthesis, a process that Morgan calls "imaginization," an attempt "to foster a kind of critical thinking that encourages us to understand and grasp the multiple meanings of situations and to confront and manage contradiction and paradox, rather than to pretend that they do not exist (p. 330).

With some effort it is easy to transfer new qualitative "human science" methods to resolving traditional library problems. In particular, the Critical Theory view of communication has substantial implications for all library activities that involve the transfer, organization, and conversion of data to information to useful information. In some cases this has already been done. For example we now recognize the distortion of cultural differences perpetuated by the Dewey Classification System. Our understanding of public libraries has been substantially enriched by the works of Harris, Garrison, Ditzion, Shera, and others.

But there are many other areas in library and information studies that are ripe for Critical Theory analysis. Just a small list would include literacy, library education, library administration, and reference work. In reference work, for example, recent study has reemphasized the problematic nature of traditional assumptions about the correctness of our practice (Hernon & McClure, 1987). Critical Theory requires a systematic questioning of our own assumptions without fear of disillusionment or criticism in an atmosphere of free and open discourse. The ultimate goal of Critical Theory is *not* to condemn but to improve.

REFERENCES

Agassi, Joseph. (1979). The functions of intellectual rubbish. *Research in Sociology of Knowledge, Sciences and Art* (Vol. 2, pp. 209–227). Greenwich, CT: JAI Press

Argyris, Cris, et al. (1985). *Action Science*. San Francisco: Jossey-Bass.

Barrell, James J. (1987). Human science research methods. *Journal of Humanistic Psychology, 27*, 451–453.

Benson, J. Kenneth. (1983). A dialectical method for the study of organizations. In G. Morgan (Ed.), *Beyond method: Strategies for social research*. Beverly Hills, CA: Sage.

Butler, Pierce. (1933). *An introduction to library science*. Chicago: University of Chicago Press.

Curran, Charles. (1988). Warning—Reading this article may be hazardous. This article contains absolutely no empirical findings. Articles with no empirical findings have been determined to cause consternation in laboratory-minded librarians. *Public Libraries, 27*, 167–168.

Daniel, Evelyn H. (1987). New curriculum areas. In R. K. Gardner (Ed.), *Education of library and information professionals* (pp. 53–70). Littleton, CO.: Libraries Unlimited.

D'Elia, George. (1988). Materials availability fill rates—Useful measures of library performance? *Public Libraries, 24*, 106–110.

Forester, John. (1985). Critical theory and planning practice. In J. Forester (Ed.), *Critical Theory and Public Life* (pp. 202–227). Cambridge, MA: MIT Press.

Forester, John. (1983). Critical theory and organizational analysis. In G. Morgan (Ed.), *Beyond method*. Beverly Hills, CA: Sage.

Geuss, Raymond. (1981). *The idea of a critical theory*. Cambridge: Cambridge University Press.

Giroux, H. (1983). *Theory and resistance in education. A pedagogy for the opposition*. South Hadley, MA: Bergin & Garvey.

Habermas, Jürgen. (1981). *The theory of communicative action* (Vol. 1). (Thomas McCarthy, Trans.). Boston: Beacon Press.

Harris, Michael H. (1986). The dialectic of defeat: Antimonies in research in library and information studies. *Library Trends, 34,* 515–531.

Harris, Michael H. (1984). Review of research in librarianship. In Mary Jo Lynch (Ed.), *Library Trends, 32.* Also in *Library and Information Science Research, 8,* 109.

Held, David. (1980). *Introduction to critical theory: Horkheimer to Habermas.* Berkeley: University of California Press.

Hernon, Peter, & McClure, Charles R. (1987). *Unobtrusive testing and library reference service*. Norwood, NJ: Ablex.

Kemp, Ray. (1985). Planning, public hearings, and the politics of discourse. In J. Forester (Ed.), *Critical theory and public life*. Cambridge, MA: MIT Press.

Lewin, Kurt. (1935). Environmental forces in child behavior and development. In D. K. Adams & K. E. Zener (Trans.), *A dynamic theory of personality: Selected papers*. New York: McGraw-Hill.

Luke, Timothy W., & White, Stephen K. (1985). Critical theory, the information revolution, and an ecological path to modernity. In J. Forester (Ed.), *Critical theory and public life*. Cambridge, MA: MIT Press.

Marchant, Maurice P., & Smith, Nathan M. (1982). The research library director's view of librarianship. *College & Research Libraries, 43,* 437–444.

Mason, Richard O., & Mitroff, Ian I. (1981). *Challenging strategic planning assumptions: Theory, cases, and techniques*. New York: Wiley.

McCarthy, Thomas. (1978). *The critical theory of Jürgen Habermas*. Cambridge, MA: MIT Press.

McClure, Charles, et al. (1987). *Planning and role setting for public libraries: A manual of options and procedures*. Chicago: American Library Association.

Morgan, Gareth. (Ed.). (1983). *Beyond method: Strategies for social change*. Beverly Hills, CA: Sage.

Morgan, Gareth. (1986). The art of organizational analysis. In *Images of organization*. Beverly Hills, CA: Sage.

Morgan, Gareth (1986—). Imagination. A Direction for the Future. In G. Morgan (Ed.), *Images of organization*. Beverly Hills, CA: Sage.

O'Neill, John. (1976). *On critical theory*. New York: Seabury Press.

Roderick, Rick. (1986). *Habermas and the foundations of critical theory*. New York: St. Martin's Press.

Rubin, Richard. (1986). *In-house use of materials in public libraries*. Urbana-Champaign: Graduate School of Library and Information Science, University of Illinois.

Sabia, R., & Wallulis, Jerald. (Eds.). (1983). *Changing social science: Critical theory and other critical perspectives*. Albany: State University of New York Press.

Samuels, Alan R. (1982). Planning and organizational culture. In C. R. Mc-Clure (Ed.), *Planning for library services: A guide to utilizing planning methods for library management* (pp. 115–150). New York: Hayworth.

Shera, Jesse H. (1970). *Sociological foundations of librarianship*. Bombay: Asia Publishing House.

Shera, Jesse H. (1972). *The foundations of education for librarianship*. New York: Becker and Hayes.

Tar, Zoltan. (1977). *The frankfort school: The Critical Theories of Max Horkheimer and Theodor W. Adorno*. New York: Wiley.

Van House, Nancy. (1985). The usefulness of fill rates. *Public Libraries, 27,* 15–32.

Wright, H. Curtis. (1986). The symbol and its referent: A Issue for library education. *Library Trends,* pp. 729–776.

12
Roads Not Taken: Some Thoughts About Librarianship

F. William Summers

School of Library and Information Studies
The Florida State University

INTRODUCTION

Over the last half century or more, librarianship in America has pursued a number of paths in various areas of the field. It will be the purpose of this essay to examine some of these paths in the light of present knowledge in order to determine whether these goals remain valid and whether some other paths which might still be taken would place the field in a stronger position.

THE SEARCH FOR LARGER UNITS OF SERVICE

Since the end of World War II, libraries in the USA, especially public libraries, have been engaged in a major effort to develop larger units of service. Fueled by Federal funds under LSCA and other programs, this effort has sought the creation of county and regional library systems across the country. These systems have taken different forms in various states but all have had the principal objective of increasing the level of services available through local libraries.

For the most part this effort has been based upon the assumption that the smaller library was inherently inefficient and could not afford to provide the full range of modern library services. These modern services were seen as including specialized staff, efficient technical services, specialized information materials, back files of periodicals and, above all, well-developed service programs for users.

The desire for larger units of service was also based upon the principle of economies of scale, that is, by spreading the costs of a specialized service or staff member over a larger number of people the cost per unit would be lowered. Thus the larger unit would not

127

only offer services which would not otherwise be economically feasible, it would also provide them at lower costs per use than could be obtained in any single, smaller library. Whether that goal has been achieved or not is arguable and merits further examination, but that is not the purpose of this discussion.

LARGER UNITS THE ANSWER?

It is worth asking if, given what we now know about computerized networks, about resource sharing and rapid delivery of information, the larger unit of service remains a viable concept. Can networks provide the basis for making the smaller library more able to offer a full range of services? There is a great deal of discussion in the literature about the ability of electronic communication and computers to overcome the restraints of distance, but we have not given the question of size the same scrutiny.

It is possible that, given sufficient expertise to access appropriate networks, the small library can obtain many of the services and much of the information which are otherwise available only at a larger system headquarters. One could suggest that size of immediately available collection is no longer the critical factor that it once was seen to be. The network can provide the same economies of scale as does the larger library system and can furnish the higher level of professional staff expertise as well.

The impact of modern technology on library system structure has not been thoroughly examined, principally because the developments of library networks occurred initially in the larger systems and not in the smaller libraries. The availability of relatively low-cost, high-capacity computer systems, however, may well have the potential to alter the most desirable configurations of library systems and should be reexamined.

THE FOCUS ON BIBLIOGRAPHY

One cannot view the efforts at library automation which have occurred over the last 30 years without becoming aware that most of this effort, and it has been a very massive effort, has been devoted to the creation in machine-readable format of bibliographic records not unlike the bibliographic records which had been created earlier in libraries. The MARC record was, and is, predominantly a recreation in machine readable form of the 7 1/2 cm. x 12 1/2 cm. card which preceded it.

While the availability of the computer certainly provided the opportunity to transfer to it the library processes then in place, it also afforded an opportunity to seek new ways to exploit the new medium and the opportunity to rethink the basic assumptions governing bibliographic records. Instead of re-examining these basic assumptions from the user's point of view, the field chose to consider them principally from the library's point of view and to adapt current operations to the computer rather than to rethink those operations from the perspective of what the computer could enable us to do that had not been done before. The decision not to provide a subject search capability in the MARC format is one such example. In a more recent decision one of the more widely used systems for public access catalogs requires users to use the precise LC subject heading in a search. If they do not they will be told that no materials exist on the subject which is entered.

Computerized bibliographic systems could easily provide users much greater flexibility than we have chosen to provide to date. The computer could, for example, interact with the user to provide much more flexibility than at present. The user could be offered additional books by the same author, or invited to explore related subjects. The process of transfer to a *see* or *see also* reference could be suggested to the user.

It is also apparent that little effort has been made to exploit the opportunity for greater subject analysis which the computer provides, at least in the systems built for libraries. Not many online systems provide for Boolean searching, nor has there been a great increase in the number or depth of subject headings assigned to books. Library cataloging, it is probably safe to assert, offers little or no greater subject depth in the post-MARC era than was available in the pre-MARC period. If one wishes in-depth subject analysis today, then one must, for the most part, go out into the private market place and purchase it from vendors who *have* filled a void the profession *chose* not to fill.

The field has chosen the path of using the computer to convert existing library operations, procedures, and concepts but has not chosen the path of fully exploring the potential which the computer has offered—to do things in a different and possibly better way. Thus library after library has gone through the laborious task of retrospectively converting to machine-readable format records for books which will not be used or which will be used with decreasing frequency. Our utilization of computers has served to glorify the art of library cataloging, but it has not taken full advantage of the potential of computers. Even after 30 years of effort we are still hard put to answer the question of whether users, as opposed to libraries, are better off because of the systems we have built.

THE PERPETUATION OF THE MASTER'S DEGREE

When in the 1920s professional education for librarianship began to move substantially into colleges and universities, it made that move at the post-baccalaureate level—initially with the old fifth year bachelors degree and subsequently with the MLS. The rationale for placing professional education at this level was that since librarians dealt with all branches of knowledge, students should not be encouraged to dilute the then-predominantly liberal arts degree with vocational courses. This position probably made the new schools much more acceptable to the traditional academic disciplines then present in universities.

The Liberal Arts Argument

The argument for the strong liberal arts preparation was perhaps valid at that time, but it has grown increasingly weaker over the ensuing years. Perhaps its weakest point is that students do not take and have not for some years taken liberal arts programs in strong numbers. They major in the undergraduate disciplines of other professions, notably education, social work, and business. What passes for liberal arts education today is a group of courses, taken generally in the first two years of college, called general education or something similar. After that time the student chooses a major and focuses the remainder of the undergraduate years on specialization courses in that major. Even those students who choose liberal arts majors receive a relatively narrow preparation in that field.

It is also the case that libraries have broadened to the point that one would be hard put to argue that liberal arts preparation is the only, or even the best, preparation for those who wish to enter the field. Given that many liberal arts majors require no more than 30–40 hours of course work, the would-be librarian could certainly have space in a sound program for an additional undergraduate major or at least a minor in the professional field. Yet the field has continued to insist that all professional study must be at the graduate level.

An Undergraduate Component

This insistence is even more difficult to defend in a period of time when the library educators are concerned that there is not sufficient time within the MLS program for the student to include all the needed courses and experiences, and in some cases schools are lengthening their programs beyond the traditional calendar year. If the curriculum needs to be expanded, there is an opportunity to consider expansion at the undergraduate level rather than the graduate. There would appear to be little intellectual or pedagogical reason why many of the basic courses required in most library schools could not easily be accommodated at the undergraduate level. If the 12–20 hours of required courses were included in an undergraduate program along with some of the kinds of prerequisite experiences which library schools would like students to have, that is, courses in computers, statistics, and mathematics, then a much stronger student would be ready to enroll in the master's degree program which could then accommodate in the 30–36 hours available the kinds of programs which many believe are important.

Creating an undergraduate major would do a great many things for the field and the library schools as well. It is well noted that library schools suffer a problem of visibility on their own campuses. Operating an undergraduate program would place the library school directly in touch with the principal activities of most universities. Library schools presently do not play much of a role in the major activities of undergraduate curricular matters such as honors courses, undergraduate registration, development of calendars, and the entire world of faculty governance of the largest sector of the university. Also the undergraduate students who will one day enroll in the library school are generally unaware of its existence because it has nothing to offer them. Having an undergraduate major would place the library school in the same business that occupies a major proportion of the time, energy, and resources of the remainder of the campus.

Today librarianship remains alone as the one field on most college campuses which has no undergraduate program. Schools of social work which used to follow the same pattern have long since moved to create undergraduate programs. Is it not time that librarianship looked carefully at the undergraduate level as the point at which the curriculum might most realistically be expanded?

THE MAINTENANCE OF THE COMMON CORE

Along with graduate preparation, librarianship has clung tenaciously to a core of required courses which is pretty much common to the various library schools. With the exception of the addition of a course in information science and, in a few instances, one in research, this core has remained essentially unchanged since the earliest days of professional education. It consists of courses in cataloging or technical services, reference or information services, book selection or collection management, library operations or management, and a catch-all course commonly called social functions of libraries, foundations of library and information science, or something similar.

The core courses are seen as playing a variety of roles in the program, all of them rather important. First, the core is a foundation upon which the student builds a specialization in some area of the field. Second, the core is designed to present those common principles and viewpoints which are deemed essential to all librarians regardless of the type of professional service which they may ultimately undertake.

As the field exists today the core presents a number of problems. First is the basic question of validity. Can there really be said to exist a body of knowledge which all librarians need regardless of their field of practice? Second, assuming a positive answer to the first question, how does that core support the efforts of library schools which are now attempting to prepare individuals for information service positions outside of libraries? Thirdly, how about the problem that the core has grown to the point that it now occupies a disproportionate part of the total curriculum? These problems are fundamental. They merit individual consideration.

The Core

Is there a basic core body of knowledge which all librarians must possess? It must be accepted immediately that whether there is such a core or not the field has functioned for a long time on the belief that there is. It must also be acknowledged that the question has never been put to any sort of valid empirical test. No one knows whether librarians who receive the normal core courses perform better than those who do not because there is simply no place in which the idea can be tested. Those who try to argue against the core immediately come up against arguments such as: "Do you believe that librarians shouldn't know 'X'?" "X" can be basic reference sources, the ability to understand LC or Dewey classification, or the difference between Theory X and Theory Y in management.

A good argument can be made for the inclusion of almost any specific piece of professional knowledge in the required body of courses. An individual could certainly argue that not everyone needs to know book selection, or that it makes little sense to teach people how to be managers when they are inevitably some years from management responsibilities, but these arguments are likely to have little relevance in discussions about curricular change because each part of the core has its adherents present in any school. In actuality what frequently occurs is a type of standoff in which no one questions another's area of the core and receives the same courtesy in return.

As library schools have also attempted to become schools of information "science," "study," or "management" and to begin the preparation of individuals for broader roles in the information service fields, the adequacy of the core of courses has been brought into sharp question. Whatever else it may be, the core is shaped to prepare people to work in libraries, and to understand the values and perspectives which drive those institutions. Persons who wish to work as information specialists or managers in industry or government find small value in courses aimed at preparing library catalogers or reference desk workers. The history of librarianship and the organization of the American Library Association have little relevance to them. Library book selection doesn't mean much to individuals who will work in organizations which do not preselect information but go out and acquire it only when it is needed. These individuals are not likely to see the relevance of these courses or express interest in enrolling in schools which require them. Adherence to the core of librarianship may prove to be a major stumbling block preventing library schools from moving into a strong position in the preparation of individuals for information service roles very different from those we customarily call library service.

The Expansion of the Core

As the field has grown and its emphases have changed, many library schools have sought to enlarge the content of the core without, in most cases, deleting anything from it. The most frequent addition has been an introductory course in information science. Such a course is usually necessary because for the most part students have come into the field with little or no appreciation of computers and their use as information-handling devices. In addition, some schools have wished to introduce a course in research into the core. These courses have varied from what might be considered a "research appreciation" approach to one which actually introduces the students to the process of research in the field. The first approach suffers from an obviously limited perspective and the second from the fact that most students come into library schools with extremely limited knowledge and skills in numerical measurement.

Nevertheless, the effort to add new content without deleting the old has generally meant an expansion of the number of required courses. Not many years ago the core of required courses normally consumed one-fourth to one-third of the student's entire program, about 9–12 hours. Now it frequently uses one-half or more of the total program, leaving the student little opportunity for in-depth specialization and virtually no opportunity to explore the field through elective courses. It is this tension which has been a major factor in leading a number of library schools to decide to lengthen their programs.

An important road not taken is that library schools have not critically examined their required core and the philosophic premises upon which it rests. It may well be that the efforts to preserve this core have been misplaced and that it will be increasingly anachronistic in the future. If the field had focused more attention on the design of the specializations in the field and much less upon the definition and preservation of the common core, it might have stronger curricula in library schools.

THE ROLE OF THE STATE LIBRARY AGENCIES

For many years the profession has expressed the belief that strong state library agencies are critical for the success of various professional goals. The literature is filled with such testimony. Yet as one examines the state library agencies across the country, it becomes clear that overall they are not very strong.

In the glow of expectancy and hope for a better, more prosperous country which accompanied the end of World War II, the profession, along with others, embraced efforts at long-range planning. This effort was aimed at ushering in an era of plenty and graciousness to a nation in which these qualities had been denied by economic upheaval and postponed by war.

In this spirit librarianship endorsed a number of planning efforts. A principal one was the Public Library Inquiry which produced several major volumes addressing a number of opportunities before public libraries. In one of those volumes, *The Public Library in the Political Process*, Oliver Garceau (1949) warned the profession not to seek broad-scale federal aid for libraries until it had taken steps to strengthen the state library agencies. It was his belief that successful local programs required the presence of strong and effective state libraries to support and direct them and to marshal the resources of the state behind local library development.

Garceau's advice was ignored and in 1955 the Library Services Act (to be followed by the Library Services and Construction Act) was passed. It is not to be argued here that these federal programs did not have significant impact upon state and local library services because clearly they did. We can, however, ask the question of whether we might not have accomplished more with these programs if the state library agencies had been in a stronger position.

One of the early issues which plagued LSCA was conflict within a number of states about how much of the federal funds should be used at the state level, to support state agency operations and state-wide services, and how much should be made available for grants to local libraries (a conflict which continues to appear from time to time). Certainly, if Garceau had been heeded, the programs and services needed at the state level would have been in place and it would have not been necessary to go through, in many cases, years of using federal funds to build state programs.

If state support for public libraries is a measure of state commitment to libraries, then we must ask from another perspective if Garceau were not correct, and if we should not have gone down a different road. If one excludes the support provided in the nine or ten best supported states (New York, New Jersey, Pennsylvania, Illinois, California, etc.), then the average state support for public libraries in the remaining 40 states is only about $1,000,000. In at least 25% of the states there is no state aid, a rather clear indication that the state library agencies have not been in a strong position to command fundamental support for library development within the states.

By contrast when the Elementary and Secondary Education Act was passed, it contained a separate title for strengthening state departments of education. Those funds were undoubtedly used in many ways, some wise and some not so wise, but the residues which one sees today in these departments are impressive. Almost all state departments of education have strong research efforts which are able to track the impact of state and local funds upon schools and to make realistic assessments of the strengths of school programs. Ongoing basic education data systems are in place which support needs assessments and funding need projections. State departments of education come much closer to having the full range of professional expertise necessary to their mission than do state libraries.

It is also clear that these stronger departments of education have been able to much more clearly establish that fundamental support of education is a state/local responsibility, with the state share growing much more dramatically than the share we have been able to achieve for public libraries.

Would things have been different and better for state library agencies and for public libraries had we followed the advice which Garceau offered? On balance the evidence seems to prompt a "yes" answer, but we did not go down that road so we cannot now know.

SPECIALIZATION VERSUS GENERALIZATION

In the early history of the profession we did not divide ourselves into specializations. Certainly until well into the 20th century a *librarian* was a *librarian* and did whatever *librarian work* came to hand. In this era one saw librarians move from academic to public to special library with ease. Thus, John Cotton Dana can be hailed as a great *public* library leader in Newark and also as a founder of the *Special* Libraries Association. By at least mid-century, however, the profession had begun to add specializations. At first these were specializations in job function only, but gradually they became specializations in educational preparation as well. At the same time we began to divide the profession into specialized groups—some, such as special librarians and law librarians, in separate organizations; others, such as public and academic librarians, under the umbrella of the American Library Association.

Now we have ever more numerous and narrower specializations. A glance at the *A.L.A. Handbook of Organization* will more than prove this point as one finds groups such as "Public Service Managers of Microform Facilities," "Technical Services Administrators of Medium-sized Research Libraries," and there is another group for "Technical Services Directors of Large Research Libraries." There are groups for school media specialists in nonpublic schools, for metropolitan libraries, for urban libraries, for rural libraries, and for small and medium-sized libraries wherever they may be.

No doubt each of these groups believes that its concerns and perspectives are unique and that if it did not address these concerns they would not be addressed. Each believes that it has or seeks special insights into its areas of concern. The validity of these assertions is not being called into question here, although it should be noted in passing that few if any of them have been subjected to any kind of empirical research. Rather, the question is: Are we as a profession better off because we have chosen to divide ourselves into narrower and narrower specializations? Are the users of libraries better off? Would our profession be stronger if we had continued to say a *librarian* is a *librarian*?

People are prepared for the generalized profession and they learn their specialization in practice. Had we followed this road, library school curricula would certainly be a great deal more straightforward, less encumbered with courses, and possibly not under pressure to expand into longer and longer programs. Those few schools which did decide to define and offer specializations would clearly have to differentiate those special preparations from their basic librarian preparation, and we might see library schools being essentially honest about what a specialization is and is not. Presently students graduate from some library schools claiming two or three "specializations" while in others they are hard put to finish one in a typical program length.

Most library educators and practitioners would agree that a specialization is something more than one course in a given area, but beyond this there is little agreement. The road not taken was the insistence upon continuing the view that a *librarian* is a *librarian*.

CONCLUSION

Ernest R. DeProspo frequently pointed out that all decisions, whether by individuals, organizations, or professions, required a choice of one alternative over another or others. They involved costs. The costs were always two kinds—the costs involved in pursuing the alternative selected and the forfeit costs of not pursuing other alternatives which might have been chosen.

In this essay, a number of choices made by the profession a long time ago and some more recent choices have been examined. It is not intended to suggest necessarily that these choices should be reversed and others made. It is often not possible to go back and travel another road. The discussion is offered to suggest a different context for looking at choices in the future. First of all, the futurity of current decisions may be much more significant than it appears to be. Each of the choices noted above was undoubtedly made for the best of motives to produce worthwhile results. Over the long run, however, it appears that other choices might have been better. At least the ability to make other choices in the future ought to have been preserved.

Second, it should be observed that in many areas choices once put in place take on a life of their own and impact upon other factors in our systems and environments in ways not intended or anticipated.

A profession can never avoid choosing between varying alternatives, choosing a road, but such choices must always be made with a view that choosing to follow one road is inevitably a choice not to proceed down another. The road not to be taken deserves perhaps as much or more scrutiny than the one which appears most pleasant or direct.

REFERENCES

Garceau, Oliver. (1949). *The public library in the political process.* New York: Columbia University Press.

13
A Biographical Sketch of Ernest R. DeProspo, Jr.

Philip M. Clark

**Division of Library and Information Science
St. John's University**

INTRODUCTION

In this short chapter I intend to reflect upon some of the major themes and ideas that Ernest R. DeProspo contributed to the field of library and information studies. As a member of the faculty at the Rutgers University School of Communication, Information and Library Studies from 1967 until his death in 1986, he was advisor, counselor, and friend to scores of doctoral and masters students, as well as international leader and proponent of ideas about management and organization of public libraries.

ERNEST R. DEPROSPO, JR.

From Public Administration to Library Studies

Ernie came to librarianship through the study of public administration. He was a research assistant at the Pennsylvania State University in the early 1960s when the Institute of Public Administration functioned as a research bureau for the Pennsylvania State Library. Ralph Blasingame was then Pennsylvania State Librarian and Ralph had contracted with the Institute and its Director, Dr. John Ferguson, to conduct a study that eventually helped define the boundaries of the Commonwealth's area library system. At the time, Ernie was a doctoral student in political science, and he was assigned to the Pennsylvania study.

I recall that Ernie was the first person I met when I arrived at the Institute in 1963 and was assigned to work with him on the study that resulted in Ken Beasley's *A Statistical Reporting System for Local Public Libraries* (1964). That study, by the way, was the direct inspiration for *Performance Measures for Public Libraries* (DeProspo, Altman, Beasley, & Clark, 1973). Ernie was also highly involved in the planning stages of the study that led to Bill Monat's *The Public Library and Its Community* (1967) although he interrupted his work on libraries for a year to do a study in Peru. DeProspo's work at the Pennsylvania State University was truly seminal. It was rich in field experience and replete with information on what public libraries were all about. Both of us eventually moved to Rutgers University, and our efforts to provide at Rutgers a research environment similar to the one we had experienced at Penn State were based upon the models developed and studies conducted there.

Penn State had educated Ernie in the rigors of political science and academic politics. Two "hot" books of this period that stayed with Ernie and influenced his teaching and thinking throughout his academic career were David Easton's *A Framework for Political Analysis* (1965) and Abraham Kaplan's *The Conduct of Inquiry* (1964). Easton's book provided a major structure for Ernie's dissertation and convinced him of the usefulness of general systems theory. The "Easton Model" became a staple in DeProspo classes, and Kaplan's book became an institutional fixture at Rutgers for all PhD students in his research methods seminars. (Indeed, Kaplan is cited often in the papers included in this collection. Ernie's students not only *remember* Kaplan, they continue to be influenced by him.) The topics of Systems Theory and Research Methodology remained constants in Ernie's subsequent work.

At Penn State Ernie had encountered academic politics and faculty internecine warfare. As I recall, he got caught in a crossfire between several senior faculty members. One battle was waged over his doctoral dissertation. Ernie survived and prevailed, and I know that some of the procedures he instituted at Rutgers, such as the formal proposal, the agreement and support of the proposal by the faculty committee, and the positive nature of the defense were all fashioned in reaction to his experiences at Penn State.

I also know that despite the few negative experiences, Ernie thoroughly enjoyed his student days at Penn State, and he sought to bring the aura of student togetherness and camaraderie we had at Penn State to Rutgers. He envisioned a full partnership between student and instructor, and I think he was a prime mover in achieving that at Rutgers.

Rutgers Days

In 1967 Ernie moved to Rutgers where Ralph Blasingame had already joined the faculty. Dean Neal Harlow had seen the need for interdisciplinary approaches to solving library service problems, spotted a talent for this approach in Ernie, and brought him on board. The Bureau of Library and Information Science Research was established, with Ralph and Ernie as co-directors and me as executive director. This Bureau was to give operational expression to Harlow's vision and it became the nerve center for Rutgers involvement in library research and problem solving. The Bureau soon began to pay its own way, became a respected unit of the library school, and acquired several important federal research contracts and a number of grants to assist the New Jersey State Library as well. Ernie also became co-chair of the Library Development Committee of the New Jersey Library Association at a time when that committee functioned as a primary professional advisory committee to the State Library.

From the beginning of his tenure at Rutgers, Ernie was involved with the doctoral program. He was a popular mentor and adviser, serving frequently as chair of dissertation committees and as a member of almost all of them. Eventually he became director of the Ph.D. Program, a position he held at his death.

Themes

Many themes run through Ernie's work. The most important and all-encompassing were accountability, objectivity, and rigor. He applied these to problems of institutional and personal performance measurement, to planning, goal and objective setting, and program evaluation. In his personal life he was loyal, candid, and a sly jester. An overriding concern of his was that people in public agencies should do well for their clients.

Accountability, objectivity, and rigor affect the reasons why we do things, the manner in which we do them, and the quality of our efforts. In public administration, the field in which Ernie was educated, the concept of keeping the public trust is a strong moral imperative. That same orientation stressed efforts to control bias and to employ empirical methods. Certainly Ernie had his likes and dislikes—he acknowledged these—but he was devoted to the discovery of truth and to expanding the limits of our knowledge.

Ernie confronted every one of his students at one time or another with this question: "What problem are you trying to solve?" In so doing he sharpened the skills of all who attempted research under his watchful eye, for he required his students to include in their problem statements a consideration of the importance of the topic proposed, its measurability, and their views as to the value of solving the problem.

Working under his direction, students often found the completion of the problem statement the most difficult of exercises. Ernie badgered them in much the same way that he badgered planners who worked with him. But no student and no planner ever got away without being able to construct solid goal statements and crisp, measurable objectives. In fact, he prepared many of his students for the planning process by forcing them to treat their problem statements the same way planners treat their concept documents and outlines of strategies. Ernie did these things well as counselor, friend, teacher, or co-worker; he assumed whatever role it took to get the message home.

What Ernie Would Emphasize

Dissertation research and program planning/evaluation are not dissimilar in terms of the techniques used to "solve" the problems they pose. The *uses* to which findings will be put may be quite different but the processes are not. This inherent commonality between the techniques of empirical research and the practice of planning can perhaps best be summarized by thinking of Ernie's emphasis on "policy value research"—that is, research that aims to answer "questions of what is to be done by people in quandaries" (Kaplan, 1964, p. 398). Ernie was adamant in his position that scientific inquiry was more than the search for abstract truth; it needed to be useful as well.

Well, by the late 1960s, a number of people in public librarianship felt that they were in a quandary when it came to describing how well they were providing library service to their clients. They had doubts about the legitimacy and persuasiveness of arguments based upon the "bigger is better" view. At that time the primary measuring device for illustrating how well a library was doing was the 1956 Minimum Standards for Public Libraries. Ernie and others criticized these standards for being derived purely on the basis of professional guesswork rather than from rigorous testing of the underlying concepts. The standards in 1966 recommended resource sharing, observing that no single unit could keep up with the volume of published materials, but nothing was devised to replace the "handy" checklist of levels of effort that was provided in the earlier standards.

The 1960s also saw the full flowering of "systems thinking" across a broad range of scientific enterprise. The pervasiveness of the movement was acknowledged by its father, Ludwig von Bertalanffy (1968): "If someone were to analyze current notions and fashionable catchwords, he would find 'systems' high on the list. The concept has pervaded all fields of science and penetrated into popular thinking, jargon and mass media" (p. 3).

Among the many concepts that came from the systems theory movement, the concepts of outputs and feedback may have the greatest utility. Systems terms allowed us to contrast the old standards with their emphasis on "inputs" to a needed emphasis on showing what the library produced—"outputs." Similarly, the presence of feedback could mean that a system was dynamic and open to change. It produced a product and used the reactions to that product to produce a new and improved version of the original. The process was observed to be neverending because the changes in the environment would require changes in the system serving it and under study.

The verification of this concept is a current reality. It is so ingrained in contemporary thinking that current observers might be tempted to think it has been with us for years. It has not. A young scholar named Ernest Deprospo is chiefly responsible for taking ideas like output and feedback and applying them to the problems of measurement and evaluation of libraries and library services.

The effort that went into *Performance Measures for Public Libraries* and dealing with the landslide reaction to that work constituted a major portion of Ernie's productive life. The book was a product of a U.S.O.E.-funded study by the Rutgers Bureau of Library and Information Science Research. In addition to Ernie, Ken Beasley, Ellen Altman, and Ellen Clark were the major staff participants.

The study was intended to create and test objective measurement tools which would allow library administrators to show that a library offered a broader array of services than was usually documented in standard reports in current use. It did this by focusing on the outputs of the process and, in particular, on how *available* those services were.

The major accomplishment of these kinds of measurement tools and procedures was that they enabled librarians to focus upon improved performance, not someone else's performance, but their own. This provided a new perspective on accountability. Demonstrating accountability would no longer be tied exclusively to the process of equaling figures achieved by other libraries in other environments but upon benchmarks and targets established at local libraries by local librarians. The monumental importance of this breakthrough in thinking—this abandoning of the "my library is as big, or isn't so big, as your library" mindset—cannot be overstated nor can Ernie's role in helping to bring it to our attention.

One critical restraint that was placed on the study (self-imposed, to be sure) was that the data collection and analysis techniques that resulted from the PMPL must be capable of being performed by local library staff. This was, in part, a recognition that no widespread collection of output level data would take place if the collection and analysis had to be performed by specialized researchers. In order to make the data "useful," certain limits were placed on what was to be collected. These limits were set in acknowledgment of the difficulties of collection and of analysis.

A key concern that tied *performance measures* together was the question of whether or not a summary measure or group measures could be developed that expressed a level of performance for a particular library in relation to other libraries. This concern originated with Ken Beasley's formulation of a statistical reporting system for Pennsylvania libraries in which he proposed a generalized model of the process. It is safe to say that the PMPL did not explicitly test that model, primarily because funding on the project ended before such a test could be conceived and executed.

"Performance measures" was the hot topic of the early 1970s. It got Ernie, his co-workers/co-authors, and Rutgers a lot of press. I think it also soured Ernie on sponsored research, and maybe on A.L.A. and U.S.O.E., too. In his view the bureaucratic hassles and the perceived restrictions on his freedom to pursue his interests and his ideas were too stifling. He eschewed the role of research director and withdrew to the role of consultant.

The ideas that were expressed in "performance measures" occasioned a great deal of debate. Despite the oft-repeated warnings by the study team, people viewed the numbers that resulted from the study as measures of *good* or *bad*. A long-range hope for the study had been to see if norms could be established, and if they could, perhaps standards could be based on those norms. But to find whether norms exist, a great number of libraries had to be studied. And that just did not happen.

What did happen was that the need for planning became quite evident. Ernie was convinced that only numbers such as those generated by performance measures were of value to planners. He was influential in getting this across, and he did so as a member of the P.L.A. Goals, Guidelines, and Standards Committee.

Then Ernie saw what he viewed to be a storm rising. A.L.A. and U.S.O.E. got involved in *A Planning Process for Public Libraries*. He said his piece and exited from establishment enterprise to find excitement in what for him would be more intellectually stimulating and less political endeavors.

In his new role he became an evaluation consultant to the College Entrance Examination Board in its efforts to provide public library services to adult independent learners. The participants in the project were a great joy to him, and much to his satisfaction, the involved libraries even began the process of forming an organization that stressed innovative approaches to public library services.

In his work with members of the public library profession, Ernie was a major force in bringing national attention to objective measurement of what libraries do and how that process is integral to a total planning process. I feel that the research orientation of the "performance measures" approach would have resulted in a much better handle on standards than that provided in the *Output Measures for Public Libraries* which has followed.

But 15 years after PMPL, we have progressed little toward showing how well libraries are doing their job. Part of the reason is that we are still unsure of what that job is.

REFERENCES

Beasley, Kenneth E. (1964). *A statistical reporting system for local public libraries.* University Park, PA: The Institute of Public Administration.

Von Bertalanffy, Ludwig. (1968). *General systems theory: Foundations, development, applications.* New York: Braziller.

DeProspo, Ernest R., Altman, Ellen, Beasley, Kenneth E., & Clark, Ellen C. (1973). *Performance measures for public libraries.* Chicago: Public Library Association, American Library Association.

Easton, David E. (1965). *A framework for political analysis.* Englewood Cliffs, NJ: Prentice Hall.

Kaplan, Abraham. (1964). *The conduct of inquiry.* San Francisco: Chandler.

Monat, William E., with the assistance of Pettit, Lawrence K., & Clark, Philip M. (1967). *The public library and its community: A study of the impact of library services in five Pennsylvania cities.* University Park, PA: The Institute of Public Administration.

14

Planning: The Key to Performance, Accountability, and Responsiveness and a Future for Libraries

Charles Curran

College of Library and Information Science
University of South Carolina

THE FUTURE

Planning: The Best Hope

The future has not happened yet. It is an idea, a concept.

Measured in time, it extends from the very next second to eternity, so there is a near future and a very, very distant future, and there are lots of points in between.

The future constitutes our only action area, yet it is an unknown. Conversely, and ironically, we can know the past intimately, but we cannot act to change it. We can only vow to study history and avoid repeating our past mistakes. History records both the admonitions to study it and our failure to keep our promises.

Our failure results neither from lack of interest nor from unwillingness to try. Thinking about the future is a favorite indoor sport of librarians. We write articles and books about the future of libraries and library services. We listen to presentations on the future of the public library. We even schedule national conferences on the topic. We define and redefine the Information Age. We take sides. We argue against the inevitability and desirability of the paperless society— using the word processor to arrange and rearrange our arguments.

This chapter shall not directly confront many of the *what ifs*? involved in futures study, but it shall address the central issue affecting the future of information services: It shall argue that the quality of library performance, accountability, and responsiveness shall determine the quality of the future for agencies whose mission it is to transfer information. This chapter shall also assert that studying, adopting, and executing a planning process provides assurances about performance, accountability, and responsiveness.

Obviously. *What* an information agency does, how cost-effectively it does the *what*, and how closely the agency matches the *what* with *whatever* its clients want are going to determine whether the agency survives and thrives. What is not so obvious is how the decision makers whose decisions will chart the course are going to act. What will they do with the *obvious*?

History reveals that librarianship, for example, has known about the obvious for years. For years library catechists have enunciated the commandment: Know your community. Is not "The right book for the right person at the right time" right up there? Never mind that no one actually believes this, but is not "The library is the heart of the (fill in the) ———." librarianship's most oft-repeated and sacred metaphor? We have known about responsiveness and we have known all about knowing the community. And we could apply precise measures to all of this, for we have had *standards*. Never mind that they were *in*put indicators, evidence of *potential* performance, accountability, and responsiveness, and not at all evidence of how well we were effecting information transfer.

No useful purpose would be served here by bashing the standards. A useful purpose would be served if it could be shown that attention to planning processes provides the best hope for coping with a future that is by definition unknown. No amount of planning will produce certain knowledge of the future. Nothing will. Planning forces us to examine options and develop alternative courses of action. Planning—and specifically the planning process—provides the best mechanism and the best hope for dealing with the future and with change. It includes a cycle of activities which arm decision makers with intelligence—information for decision making and for determining reactive and proactive strategies for dealing with change. Judging from the present, and the past, the future holds lots of change. Maybe the futurists have a useful message for us.

WHAT FUTURISTS DO

Futurists help us plan to intervene in the future. They provide strategies for taking advantage of good things and avoiding some of the negative consequences of bad things. They do not predict the future; they forecast the future. A prediction is a claim to know, and they make no such claim. A forecast is an opinion about the future, and informed opinions are what futurists seek; they attempt to gather as much reliable information as they can about likely and desirable futures.

The Delphi study. The tools they use, such as Delphi techniques and the cross-impact matrix, assist them in their efforts to forecast and spark movement. Delphi procedures involve the identification of questions to investigate, the identification and assembly of experts and change agents who have informed opinions about the questions, and the orchestration of reaction to the likelihood–unlikelihood and desirability–undesirability of possible future events.

The Delphi studier usually conducts the procedures by mail, for the intention is to preserve the anonymity of participants. The assumption is that anonymity protects the process from being unduly influenced by the reputations or forces of character of acknowledged experts. While participants get to exchange opinions and reactions to reactions during the Delphi rounds, they supposedly do not learn the identity of the other participants.

As experts the participants bring informed opinions to the Delphi study. As leaders and change agents they take back to the institutions and environments from which they come the processed opinions about likely–unlikely and desirable–undesirable futures. Of course procedural methods, such as selecting the right questions and assembling qualified participants, will affect the usefulness of Delphi studies, and some critics observe that Delphi procedures often require participants to consider events as isolates—single occurrences with no antecedents and no impact on other events.

The Cross-impact matrix. Futurists also employ the cross-impact matrix, which deals with this problem of relationships among possible futures. Matrix methods involve subjecting possible future events to scrutiny, within a context of the relative strength of enabling and disenabling antecedent events. For example, urban crime may be studied and forecast after a consideration of other related factors: poverty, employment, incarceration, rehabilitation, recidivism, and urban crowding. Cross-impact matrix methods include factoring in probability figures and usually involve the computer. They provide a higher order of intelligence for decision makers.

Planners as futurists. Perhaps some of us have not thought of ourselves as futurists. We may not have demythologized futures study and still retain views of crystal balls and tea leaves. But anyone who purchases an annuity or health insurance is a futurist. Futurists aim at taking advantage of opportunity and avoiding the more drastic consequences of undesirable events, and that is exactly what we hope our annuities and policies do for us. Futurists use systematically collected data to help them spot trends, and that is exactly what library decision makers who employ planning process methods do.

Planning methods demand that planners gain accurate views of current conditions and reliable forecasts of likely futures. Moreover, the planning process is *about* performance, accountability and responsiveness.

The assertion here is that planning procedures offer the best hope for a healthy library of the future. Planning procedures are futures-oriented activities which supplement impression and intuition with systematically gathered data. Performance, accountability and responsiveness are part of the fabric of planning, and the very steps of planning provide both a rationale and strategy for action, and a record of performance, accountability and responsiveness.

A CONTEXT FOR PLANNING

The fundamental principle that libraries exist to serve their communities can be illustrated with the Inner-Outer Environment Model, presented in Figure 14.1.

In the Inner-Outer Environment Model the larger outer circle represents the community. *Community* is a generic term and it consists of all the persons who have rightful access to a library's materials and services. The community circle is open in spots to allow for decisions to modify or enlarge the library's service area; through system membership, for example, or by extending user services to nonresidents who pay a fee. While the outer environment appears to have some

Figure 14.1.   The Inner-Outer Environment Model.

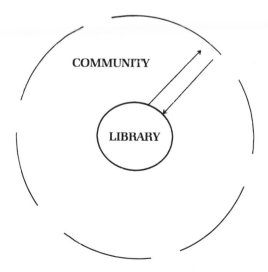

geographical properties, its essential feature is a concept of community in which rightful access is the defining, and user enfranchising, idea. *Every* library, therefore, has an outer environment, a community served.

The inner circle in the Model represents the library: its materials and services; its administration, systems and staff. A library exists in its community for the purpose of meeting the information wants and needs of the community.

Arrows point from the library to its community and from the community to the library. The arrows from the library represent materials and services, and they also represent systematic efforts to gather intelligence, conduct public relations, publicize, and market. The arrows from the community represent feedback to the library, responses to the library's programs, services, and materials.

Ideally, the arrows form a communications loop of continuous contact. And there should be multiple arrows from the library, arrows aimed at multiple targets of opportunity.

None of this targeting of services and gathering of feedback happens by chance. It must be engineered—orchestrated. A library staff designs its response to a community when they engage in the planning process. The desired relationship represented by the Model is forged by planners who invest both in the central notion of the Model—that libraries exist to serve the educational, inspirational, and recreational information needs of their communities—and in the central notion of the planning process—that librarians conceive and deliver responses based upon a process which includes looking around; figuring out what business the library is in; establishing roles and mission; designing goals, objectives and tactics; executing; and evaluating—the stuff of the planning process.

RESPONSIVENESS

Responsiveness, then, is a concept having several added dimensions. In addition to the notion of addressing an expressed or interpreted need, responsiveness includes the obligation to discover those needs, design ways to address the needs, and then interpret the Outer Environment reaction. Measuring user satisfaction may provide a partial view of how clients perceive the library response to demands placed to the system, but the concept of responsiveness, based upon the philosophical position contained in the Inner-Outer Environment Model and upon the procedural format of interrelated steps which form the planning process, is a more elaborate and useful concept.

Knowing how well libraries now serve users, apparently pretty well if we are to believe the results so far, is a good-to-know thing. Knowing that users have kind words for the library even when the library has not been able to meet requests, and knowing that users constitute only a fraction of the community—Outer Environment—prompts planners to acknowledge that survival in the future depends upon matching programs and services with the information needs of a larger portion of the community. Again, this is the essence of Responsiveness, and Responsiveness is futures-oriented and planning-dependent.

ACCOUNTABILITY

A likely future for the public library will include the obligation to keep the public trust, to make a number of promises, to deliver on promises made and to demonstrate a record of doing so.

Being accountable and *demonstrating* accountability are obviously related; the former refers to a process of performing in a responsible and responsive manner and to holding oneself answerable to the public and to public authority, the latter to a process of communicating to the public and to public authority a record of responsible service.

Planning processes, because they focus upon systematically appraising community characteristics and needs and upon establishing mission, roles, goals and objectives, strategies and tactics, and evaluation procedures, offer the best hope for public agencies to *be* accountable.

Because planning processes also focus upon the reporting of planning activities, they offer the best hope for librarians and others to *demonstrate* accountability—to communicate to funding agencies, persons of influence, and all citizens the record of performance, accountability, and responsiveness.

Telling the story in language that the bottom-liners and MBOists in city hall and county council accept and understand is an imperative. Because planning processes produce action strategies and evaluative procedures that are based upon clearly established goals and objectives, and because they provide guidance and tutoring on how to report these accomplishments, the steps of the planning processes also provide the best hope for *telling the story*.

The competition for scarce resources is not limited to city hall and county council, it is waged just as fiercely in the *reading rooms* of philanthropic organizations and federal funding agencies. Shall librarians enter this competition literate in the language of accountability? Shall they argue the cases for their information agencies as well as advocates for recreation and tourism argue for theirs? They shall if they speak *planning*.

This is not meant to suggest that the prizes will be awarded only to those who follow certain procedures, or that following certain procedures will assure success in the effort to win funding. The political process shall continue to be a political process as long as human beings exist in the human condition. In the year 2020 County Commissioners in County A are still likely to respond to a request for additional funding with the question: "What are they doing over in County B?" And decisions about granting increases to the library may be influenced by how convincingly the advocates of agencies X, Y and Z have argued their cases. The point is: The cases of rivals shall be argued in *planning-speak*, not *standards-speak*.

PERFORMANCE

What shall librarians perform in the future; how shall they perform; and how shall this performance be judged?

If libraries provide what people want in the way of information services, libraries and librarians will survive and thrive in the future. If librarians are perceived as providers of information people want, or if they are perceived as essential links between people and the information people want, librarians have a promising future. The information explosion, the complexity explosion which has led to the geometric increase in specialties and specialists, and the proliferation of data bases have combined to render the pinpointing and delivery of relevant information a difficult and useful skill—a skill which must become associated with the craft of librarianship.

Librarians who do not manage these kinds of services, who perform as custodians rather than as suppliers, who overemphasize educative responsibilities and underemphasize delivery, who pursue the goals of the bibliographic instructionists instead of the goals championed by advocates of information literacy, who define *information* too narrowly, who think they have to resolve the silly question of quality versus demand (instead of just catering to *both* in response to community tolerances), who systematically exclude themselves and their libraries from the political process, will preside over institutions destined for the scrap heap or, worse, for the scavenger's existence, nature's and society's penalty imposed upon organisms which do not evolve.

THE NEW TECHNOLOGY AND THE FUTURE

Divided Ranks

The information professions appear to be divided about new technology issues. Some school media specialists have sought an identity free of association with the word *library.* They do not want to be called librarians anymore because they believe the word conjures up unfavorable images and dated services. They want to be identified with media of all types and with computer hardware and software. Librarians, especially academic and public varieties, want to embrace the new technology and to be observed in the process of doing so, but in some of their libraries the fact that *information* is available via machine searched data bases is a well-kept secret. What they proudly display, instead, are automated inventory control processes like computerized acquisition and circulation operations and screen versions of card catalogs—great for in-housekeeping but only indirectly related to the process of placing into the hands of inquirers the information they need. Special librarians practice a distancing behavior which includes entertaining each other with assurances that unlike the *other* librarians, they are indeed special, as are their materials, services, clients, and attitudes toward technology. People who call themselves information managers do not really acknowledge kinship with librarians. They view their function as acquiring, producing, managing, and distributing information, a function calling for subject knowledge and use of state-of-the-art communications technologies, not the pointing and setting performed by librarians; and for the development of proactive strategies, not the passive and reactive responses perpetrated by their distant and disowned cousins, the librarians of all or any stripes. Some people who call themselves information scientists are as fascinated by machines and machine applications as they are by the properties of information.

They all want to be associated with the new technology. They are all protective of their respective turfs. They all like to boast that they are just a little bit hipper, sometimes a lot hipper, than those "other" librarians and information people. They all have their own professional organizations because the other organizations do not address their concerns squarely enough. Incidentally, one of those professional organizations fully endorses and supports its members' interests in the new technology but admonishes them not to pass along to users any charges for technologically enhanced services.

There is no reason why these organizational species need to be united any more than they now are. After all, this is the age of specialization. If they wanted to, they could even share resources while still observing the pecking orders they have established. The future can be just as bright for the school people as it can for the academics and specials. Each has its own constituency and its own mission and agenda. The assertion here is that those agenda must include methodologies for determining how to serve those respective constituencies. Methodologies most likely to help librarians and other information professionals make such judgments are offered in planning process procedures.

Librarians who employ planning processes diligently can effect the delivery of responsive services, can monitor and communicate accountability, and can make the best uses of technology in the performance of their mission.

FROM ABSTRACTION TO OPERATION

The Inner-Outer Environment Model is an abstraction which graphically illustrates a philosophy—a way of looking at things. Its essential message is: Libraries exist to serve their communities and librarians have the obligation to offer programs which clearly match community interests and needs. As an abstraction, however, the Model supplies only the message, not the methodology for acting upon the message.

It is the planning process which gives operational expression to the philosophy advanced by the IOEM. The planning process forces librarians to ask and answer the question: "What business are we in?" The planning process supplies the techniques for looking around the inner and outer environments in a systematic manner; for appraising need; for developing target-focused goals, objectives and action strategies; for evaluating those efforts; and for reporting results to the community.

SOME PROTECTIONS AFFORDED BY THE IOEM AND PLANNING PROCEDURES

The single greatest advantage of the Inner-Outer Environment Model is that it focuses the attention of planners upon the community. The view is a holistic one, and it helps put planners on notice that many factors, not just the availability of information technology, will determine the extent to which information is sought and used.

Those factors include education, condition of employment, agency and group membership, the availability of other sources of information, age, and lifestyle. These factors affect information *use*. New technologies affect information *availability*. Though related, they are not the same. *Thinking* they are the same, or that technology alone, not lifestyle, will drive use, some planners seem to want to describe the world in terms of machine and technological applications. For example, in the 1950s some library forecasters claimed the evolution of microform technology pronounced a death sentence for printed books. Attention to planning processes can help librarians check bandwagon approaches and achieve productive balance between technology and community characteristics.

The single greatest advantage planning procedures have over each and every one of the fixes, quick and not so quick, which have come before is that the planning process assumes or pre-supposes no answers. Despite occasional protestations to the contrary by their creators and adherents, the standards were equated with *goodness*. Standards brought libraries up to standard—up to goodness. When librarians were overcome by a galloping sense of social responsibility, then teen dances and way-outreach were the answers. When libraries were assumed to be the "People's Universities," that was the answer. Chaining books was once the answer. So was kidnaping scholars and making them copy holy books.

Advocates of planning processes claim their methodologies answer two related and very important questions:

1. What is it we are supposed to be doing around here?
2. How are we doing so far?

Performance, Accountability, and Responsiveness hinge on successfully answering those questions. The library's future will be defined by efforts to achieve excellence in those three areas.

THE MATURIZATION OF NEWER, QUALITATIVE METHODS

Unlike the advocates of quantitative standards and other indicators of goodness, the developers of planning process methodology have taken their time and tested their tools. Their models emerge from a considerable amount of hard work by many people. The performance measurement insights and designs provided by DeProspo, Altman, and the Clarks in their pioneering activities of the early 1970s have helped underpin the planning and output measurement work done by McClure, Zweizig, Lynch, Van House, and Rodger. Community Analysis procedures developed by Greer and Hale fit nicely into *looking-around* steps in planning processes. The American Library Association, and especially the Public Library Association, have provided essential support. The planning models now available have emerged from a decade-and-a-half of scrutiny, testing, and analysis, processes which continue and which help make the models useful and doable. They make sense because they focus upon how individual information agencies match their materials and services with known community characteristics and appraised need. They will survive in the future because they are organic and responsive.

They will, that is, if they are artfully executed. There are librarians who in their hunger for *something that works* will speed up the planning, maybe take some short cuts, or eliminate a few essential procedures altogether, or, worst of all, abandon the necessary thread that must weave through each of the steps in a process. It is not uncommon, for example, for librarians to yield to the temptation to put aside the data gathered while *looking around* and move ahead with the next step, unmindful of how the characteristics of a community ought to influence the establishment of roles. The problem is not at all with the sequence but with the trouble some of us have with merging the kinds of *soft* data that result from an inspection of the community and the kinds of *hard* data available from body counts and circulation counts.

They will survive if the planning procedures are treated with respect. Treat planning procedures like unnecessary and unmanageable rituals that will reveal nothing except what is already known and they will not survive. Give them reluctant, half-hearted attention and they will not survive. Treat them like fads, like *therapies du jour*, or like instant self-help remedies and they will not survive.

PLANNING: QUICK FIX OR LASTING REMEDY?

In *Making the Future Work* John Diebold (1984) shares an opinion and poses an interesting question in the preface to a chapter entitled, "Unleashing Innovation in Public Services":

> Many of the most important activities of our society—education, public transport, housing, the running of cities—are characterized by their labor intensiveness, lack of reliance on technology, and an incentive structure that discourages innovation and risk taking . . . . Consequently the cost of public services spirals steadily upward, while the quality and range of services declines. No . . . *new management tech-*

nique [emphasis mine] is going to reverse this continuing erosion . . . . Could the injection of market forces into public-service delivery release the energy, imagination and drive of our human resources and change this gloomy trend? (p. 151)

The search by information professionals in public service for a metaphor for *profit* will probably continue into the future. Aping the behavior of their cousins in the business world has long been a goal of librarians convinced of their inability to measure their own performance and envious of the apparent ease with which the for-profit folks measured theirs.

Planning processes offer the best hope for librarians with these kinds of yearnings. As isolates, measures like visits per capita and user satisfaction have not provided the sought-after metaphor. *Time* might. Roger Greer and others have advanced this notion. The extent to which users are willing to invest their time in partaking of what the library has to offer might describe a library's *profit*. Time is a precious commodity, and time gets more precious all the time. To what extent will citizens trade their most precious commodity for what the library has to offer?

Planning processes offer the best hope for finding out what clients want and will use. Planning processes offer the best hope for measuring the extent to which librarians can respond to clients. Planning processes offer the best hope for communicating with clients and funding agencies. Planning processes offer the best hope for librarians who seek to Perform in a Responsive and Accountable fashion.

REFERENCES

Diebold, J. (1984). *Making the future work. Unleashing our powers of innovation for the decades ahead*. New York: Simon and Schuster.

Epilogue

Ernest R. DeProspo, in the words of Phil Clark, was a "sly jester." He was a jester because he loved to laugh, especially at ruffled feathers and pomposity. He was sly because he could often get others to create the jokes for him to laugh at. I was one of the "others."

I want to tell you about some of those times so you will know about them, and about Ernie. You should know that in addition to being a man of great intensity and passion, he was one of the laughers.

Ernie made me tell an awful joke at my dissertation defense. I got to practice my defense the day before in his master's research methods class, where I gave a forgettable performance—forgettable except for the joke, which Ernie did not forget. The next day he interrupted me during my defense introduction and said, "Charles, tell us the story about Smitty."

Here I can not tell you the story about Smitty, but I can tell you the punch line. It was: "That's Smitty, and he doesn't go for that stuff, either."

I guess I *should* tell you that the setting of the story was a sporting house.

Now I remember that originally I had thought the story fit well with my dissertation conclusions: that you can't superimpose a system upon another system with unresolved system problems and expect favorable results. I figured Ernie would like that and appreciate the fact that his student was able to apply one of his favorite concepts—systems theory—to a cat house. What I did *not* count on was the looks I got from some of the guests, obviously nonsystems thinkers, at the defense.

I think that Ernie, sly jester that he was, counted on that all the time.

I also think he sent Ralph Blasingame to the faculty lounge to yank my chain after the defense. I was pacing that room, into which I had been sent to await the decision of my captors, when RB appeared.

"What's the verdict?" I asked, trying to sound confident.

"Verdict? What verdict? It's 11:30."

"But what about my dissertation?"

"I don't know about that," explained Ralph, "but it's 11:30 and 11:30 is lunchtime. You can defend a dissertation any time, but lunchtime is lunchtime."

I went to lunch with a bunch of *sly jesters* that day. Committee members Mott, Blasingame, and Chairman DeProspo. Somewhere between the pea soup and his chicken roll and swiss cheese sandwich, Ernie grinned and said, "Congratulations, Dr. Curran."

The wait was worth it.

* * *

I was fascinated to learn what made Ernie laugh. He was a good laugher. It was human foibles which amused him most—his own and others' of his acquaintance. He got a kick out of my negotiations with General Mills. General Mills made "Chippos," a potato snack that I had invested in. On the side of the box a guarantee promised money back to anyone who could honestly say that "Chippos" were not the best potato snack he ever ate.

I figured a way to get free "Chippos," told Ernie about it and received considerable encouragement from him. So I wrote the company, telling them that if they promised money back to a *dis*-satisfied customer, they ought to do something nice for a satisfied customer—me. I daydreamed about a case of "Chippos" and shared my vision with my major professor.

They sent me a recipe for peach cobbler.

Ernie made me tell that story more often than the one about Smitty.

* * *

At informal gatherings at A.L.A. meetings, Ernie always drew a crowd. I have never known anyone who commanded as much attention at the Mid-Winter and Annual Conventions. He couldn't walk down a hall without being accosted by librarians who wanted to pick his brain, mostly about measurement matters. So these informal meetings, mostly in bars, were special treats for me because of all the people I would get to meet.

Anyhow, at these sessions Ernie always made me tell about two stories I had written (To this day they remain unpublished, but for the life of me I'll never understand why.), one about a bonus baby librarian, and the other about the invention of the shopping bag. The Bonus Baby was this guy who was such a whiz in library school—he had memorized all the pious sayings like: "The right book for the right person at the right time"—that directors from all over the country vied to sign him. One sent a "sitter" to stay with the librarian until he signed a contract, but the sitter scared Bonus Baby so thoroughly that he jumped out the window of his dorm room, caught a train to Wisconsin, and got a job in a sausage factory.

That cracked Ernie up.

So did the story of the shopping bag, invented at the first A.L.A.

meeting by a Gaylord Mending Demonstration guy when he saw a lady struggling with her bag full of free exhibit brochures. He sewed handles on the bag with his Gaylord Mender. The rest is history.

* * *

Ernie was a sports enthusiast and a loyal Nittany Lion. I think he put up with me chiefly because I had taught spelling to Ted Kwalick at Montour Jr.–Sr. High School. Ted became a super tight end at Penn State and an All-Pro in the National Football League. He was a sure-handed pass catcher, a great blocker, and a deadly speller. My role in Kwalick's development was appreciated by the Professor.

On the occasions when Ernie came to South Carolina to "kibitz" with Bill Summers, the three of us would manage to get some tennis in. Ernie was an average player at best, but he was not fond of losing, and he was *determined* not to lose to a spelling teacher. He had an assortment of head games in his arsenal of weapons. Someday I am going to look in the rule book to see if it is permissible to laugh when another guy is trying to serve. Also, I'm not sure an opponent is allowed to stand in the service area to await the serve, thus blocking the server's view of legal territory and forcing him to try to avoid serving to a pair of sneakers.

I loved being around Ernie. He was so intense, yet he was a great laugher. He would laugh at me now if he knew I was unsure about the propriety of including this reminiscence in an otherwise serious collection of essays. I *know* he would. And I know he would egg me on.

"Charles, tell them about Smitty."

Charles Curran
January 1989

Author Index

Italics indicate bibliographic citations.

Subject Index